MW00774567

< 1%

Dana Kelley Bergman

ISBN 979-8-88685-693-4 (paperback)
ISBN 979-8-88832-784-5 (hardcover)
ISBN 979-8-88685-694-1 (digital)

Copyright © 2023 by Dana Kelley Bergman

All rights reserved. No part of this publication may be reproduced, distributed, or transmitted in any form or by any means, including photocopying, recording, or other electronic or mechanical methods without the prior written permission of the publisher. For permission requests, solicit the publisher via the address below.

Christian Faith Publishing
832 Park Avenue
Meadville, PA 16335
www.christianfaithpublishing.com

Printed in the United States of America

Use extreme caution when venturing into the high mountains;
severe injury or death could occur!

CHAPTER 1

As a person who is not a writer but who has a story to tell, I will do the best I can. So here we go.

I was born in Caribou, Maine my family moved to DuBois, Pennsylvania, when I was only a few months old. DuBois is a small town in the west Central Mountains of Pennsylvania. I grew up mostly in a single-parent home as my parents separated and finally divorced when I was less than a year old. I have two sisters from that relationship, Karen and Bonnie. Karen is the oldest by three years, Bonnie is a year older than me. Our mother got remarried when I was four years old to my brother Scott's dad, he was born when I was five.

My stepdad was a hardworking man who had a couple of jobs. He drove school buses on weekdays when school was in and did mechanic work on them at times on the weekends. If he wasn't working on them on the weekends, he was driving for school activities, such as sporting events, field trips, and class trips. He also worked second shift at a pressed metals factory on weeknights. He was a busy man, my mom worked full time for a department store at the customer service desk both weekdays and weekends. Needless to say, we were unsupervised most of the time. My mom and stepdad divorced when I was a sophomore in high school.

As a kid, I was always outside playing with my friends. Much of that time was spent in the woods. We built cabins of all sorts to hang out in. Some were just one-room structures aboveground. Then there were treehouses, most of them were nothing more than a platform with walls and a shed roof. One neighbor built a two-story treehouse in the woods behind my house that was a work of art. It had a door, windows, a staircase from the first floor to the second floor, and it was roomy. We built an underground cabin too, with a tunnel entry. That entry led to a one-room area that actually had a wood burner in it. As kids, we considered these our hunting camps!

Pennsylvania has a rich hunting heritage. Deer hunting in Pennsylvania is big. Season came in the Monday after Thanksgiving weekend. Schools were closed, mostly because no one was going to be there anyhow with it being deer season. Some would miss the entire week to hunt, others a day or two. In those days, many families relied on deer season to put meat on the table for their families throughout the year. When I was a kid, you were allowed to get your hunting license when you were twelve, you had to take a hunter safety course to be able to get your license. All of my buddies got their licenses when they were twelve, I didn't get mine till I was thirteen. The main reason was I had no one to take me. You couldn't hunt by yourself until you were sixteen, but I was hoping since I had mine, I may get an invite from one of my friends and get to go.

My stepdad hunted every year on opening day, but that was pretty much it. During the time he was married to my mom, I never knew of him to harvest a deer. To the best of my knowledge, he never did. I can remember thinking, *Man, it must be hard to bag one!*

There was a family that lived a couple of houses away from my house, the Royers. They were and still are a family of hunters—six kids, mom and dad, who counted on deer meat to help feed the family with that many mouths to feed. They always came home with deer. When deer season rolled around, and they were out hunting, I would keep a watch out the front door for their return. As soon as I saw their Jeep Wagoneer pull in by their garage, I would throw on my coat and boots, and out the door I would go to see what they had harvested.

Going up there to see what they had bagged and hearing the stories of the day's hunt really stirred something inside of me, right to the very core of me. It made me want to hunt even more. I'm not sure if it was the challenge of wondering if I could do it or maybe the thought of harvesting a deer and being able to feed myself and my

2

family that appealed to me at first. I know now that it was both, with the challenge of it being the part I like most.

When I was thirteen, I got a Mossberg 20-gauge bolt-action shotgun for Christmas. To say I was excited would be an understatement. The gun had a three-shot capacity, with one round in the chamber and a two-shot clip. The barrel had a "select choke" on the end. That choke gave you the option to shoot regular shot shells of pellets, as a regular shotgun, as well as the option to go to "improved cylinder" to be able to shoot slugs used for deer hunting!

The day after Christmas, my friends and I went hunting for small game, thanks to the Royers having a handful of 20-gauge shells they were willing to give me, so I had ammo. We returned with no game harvested and no shells left for me. Not that I had missed any game but because I had to let my new gun "bark"! I had shot at some cans found along the way and can say I hit my intended targets. I let my mom know when I got home I was going to be needing a box of shells to keep me in the field, which she got for me.

My mom never had the money to give us everything she would have wanted, but she did the best she could based on what she had. We always had a roof over our heads, food on the table, clothes on our backs, but most of all, we always knew we were loved. In our house, you never parted company with my mom without a hug, a kiss, followed by an "I love you." That was because none of us ever know when it may be the last time we see one another. It was that way with her until her passing.

The year rolled along, spring, summer, and into fall, which leads to hunting season. As I said, my stepdad was always busy, and I didn't get to go out hunting in buck season. However, I had applied for a doe tag and was fortunate enough to have received one. Not only did I get a doe tag, I also got an invite from the Royers to tag along with them and go doe hunting! I could hardly believe my luck.

My mom got me a box of slugs for my gun. They come five to a box. Up to that point, I hadn't shot any and wanted to make sure how they traveled out of the gun. Slugs are heavy, and they fly pretty flat for a little way, but the farther they travel, the more they drop off. For my 20-gauge, they flew pretty true out to fifty yards; after

3

that, they dropped like a rock off a cliff! I had shot at a large box at fifty yards and had shot well. I used all five of my shells and, with the drop-off, thought I should take a good supply of them just in case; you never know.

I had a paper route as a kid to help out with finances and had squirreled away a small stash of cash. I gave my mom enough money to get me five boxes of shells. *Twenty-five shots should be enough to get the job done*, I thought.

Before you knew it, the first day of doe had arrived. I woke up and got dressed. My hunting clothes were some hand-me-down Woolrich gear the neighbor, Mr. Brown, had given me. He gave me the coat and pants. They were a bit big on me, but one thing for sure was I wasn't going to get cold! I had suspenders on the pants to hold them up, and the coat hung on me a bit, but I looked the part. Mom made me something to eat, packed me a lunch, and a thermos of hot chocolate. I gathered up my gear, and out the door I went.

When I got up to the Royers' house, Mike met me at the door. Mike and I are the same age. As I said, there are six kids in the Royer family, and of those six, there are four that are the ages of me and my siblings. We all ran with our counterparts back in the day. The house was abuzz with activity, and soon we were all stacked up in the Jeep Wagoneer and off to Anderson Creek to start the day.

We arrived and parked the jeep. Once everyone rolled out, we had a huddle and talked about where everyone would be going to post up to start the morning. It was at that time I realized I would be sitting by myself. I was a little concerned because I wasn't familiar with the woods, but I set out down an old logging road and found a stump. I knocked the snow off of it and sat down. As the morning sun started to rise higher and higher, and it got lighter bit by bit, the excitement grew with each increase in the light. I find that to still be the case to this day.

Then you hear that first shot; sometimes off in the distance, sometimes so close it startles you. The world was waking up, and the shots were picking up. Then shortly after full light, I saw a lone doe about forty yards out, coming up the hill to my left. I raised my gun, took aim, and shot. Then again and again! The doe was gone, up and over the hill. The gun was empty, and I was shaking so bad from buck fever I was glad I was sitting down because I might have fallen off my feet if I was standing.

I was down because of my missed chance at the doe and, at the same time, so excited to have had the chance. I had heard of *buck fever* but, until that very moment, had no idea what it actually was. Now I knew firsthand what it was, and knew it was for real! Your heart rate picks up, your breathing becomes irregular, you get tunnel vision, and your mind is clouded making it hard to focus on the task at hand. The other thing I knew after that encounter was I loved it, deer hunting and everything about it! I knew at that very moment I was hooked and would be a deer hunter for life.

We all met sometime later, and I shared my story with every-one. I knew they could all see the disappointment on my face at my blown chance. Ginger, my second mom, whom I call Mom to this day, said, "It's okay, kid. You'll get another chance." I don't think I was as sure as she was, but I sure hoped she was right.

We loaded up and headed for another spot. When we got there, we unloaded and were all moving off into the woods, talking softly about when to meet back at the Jeep, when shots erupted across the road. We all stopped and spread out through the woods and waited.

John, who is Mike's dad, said, "Here they come."

I could see a deer headed our way, then another, then a few more. The next thing I knew, there were twenty to thirty more headed our way. I was amazed! I'm not sure who shot first, but in short order, it was on! There were deer moving everywhere, the bunch of us all shooting. I know I was seeing deer going down, but none by my hand. Another three rounds of ammo launched into the great obliv-ion. I reloaded again. Mike and I were moving through the woods when we saw a deer close. I asked Mike if he would let me shoot it. He said, "You're going to have to. I'm out of bullets." I took aim with a tree for a rest, squeezed the trigger, and the deer fell.

I couldn't believe it. I had just bagged a deer on my first hunt! I couldn't wait to get home and show my mom. I was so happy and proud! I was happy Mike was out of bullets, happy I had bought twenty-five rounds of ammo, happy I got the invite, happy I got one.

5

I couldn't thank God and the Royers enough. It meant the world to me.

That day, we all got a deer by the end of the day. When we got back to the Royers' house, Mike helped me get the deer down to my house. I can remember the look on my mom's face when I burst into the house and exclaimed, "I got one!" She seemed a bit surprised and came out to look at my trophy.

The next look on her face was one of, what are we going to do with it, since no one had ever got a deer in our house before. We sure didn't know how to butcher a deer. Mom called a place in Falls Creek, a small town a few miles away where my grandmother lived. We got directions to the place from the owner. I was excited because I figured we could swing by Nana's house and show her before dropping it off at the butcher.

We got the deer in the trunk of the old Plymouth Fury and headed over the road. It would be fair to say that my grandmother didn't share in the excitement over my achievement as much as I did once we got to her house. I do know she was happy for me and proud of me.

CHAPTER 2

My grandmother, or Nana as I referred to her earlier, always would have us come over to her place, all of us at once and sometimes just one at a time. She would make sure that she made us each feel special and spoiled us a bit in the process. She would do whatever she could to lift us up.

I also remember that she bought me my first bow-and-arrow set. I was always watching westerns as a kid and was intrigued by the marksmanship of the Indians with the bow. It wasn't a real go-hunting type of a bow, it was one of those single white pieces of fiberglass that came with three arrows equipped with suction cups on the end of them.

I was about eight at the time, but to me, it was the real deal! I would spend hours outside with it in awe of the mystical flight of the arrow. I would set up Johnny West, who was an action figure like G.I. Joe except he was a cowboy. It was me against him and all of his cowboy friends, and it was war!

I would shoot them all down, set them back up, and repeat that over and over all day long. To me, it was great fun but still lacking in some way. That something to me was being able to see my arrow actually stick in something.

One day, I found myself with a bit of "free time" at Nana's and took my three arrows to the laundry room where there was a pencil sharpener. I popped off the suction cups and did a little upgrade. I made myself some hunting arrows. I poked holes through the suction cups so I could put them back on when I came inside to keep my upgrade secret from Nana.

When I went outside, I popped them off, and in my pocket they would go. I still waged war on Johnny West and his gang, but now I spent half my time shooting at dandelions. Sometimes I hit them, sometimes I wouldn't. Didn't matter to me because the arrow was sticking in the ground, and that was cool.

My love for and interest in archery and bow hunting only grew from there and has become a lifelong passion of mine.

When my siblings and I were kids and would spend the night at Nana's house, one constant thing was at bedtime, we always said our prayers. I know when I got to the part "and God bless..." I could get long winded, but I didn't want to let anyone out. Nana just let me roll, it was my prayer, and she let it be. Nana had a deep belief in God and Jesus, and it always made me feel better to say my prayers before bed because there was always, and still is, so much to pray for.

When I was twelve or thirteen, I got another upgrade. I bought a recurve bow. It too was fiberglass, green in color. It looked like a giant piece of mint taffy. If you ever shot archery in gym class, then you know exactly what it looked like. It had enough power to hunt small game and, as far as I was concerned, deer too. It had a four-arrow Quickie Quiver attached to the limbs. When I needed anything for it, I would ride my bike into town about two miles to the archery shop. The ride would take anywhere from ten to thirty minutes, depending on if I wanted to jump my bike over the dirt piles down by the railroad tracks on the way there or on the way home.

The shop was Beezers Archery. I loved going there and looking around. There were deer racks and mounts to look at. I would always think to myself, *One day, I'm going to bag a big buck with my bow.* I wasn't sure when, but I knew it would happen.

My friends and I would go out hunting, without the slightest clue of what we were doing. Nevertheless, every time we went, we were sure this time was going to be the time. We would climb trees and sit on limbs, or if we were lucky, we may stumble onto someone's old wooden tree stand, and crawl up into it, then lay in wait for our prey. We never wore any type of fall restraint that was tethered to the tree to stop us, if by some strange chance we would fall. I never go without one now and haven't for decades, but back then, "Who's going to fall anyhow, right?" As unsafe as all that was, to heighten the danger, my quiver on my bow didn't have a hood on it. The hood is a cover that your arrows sink into that holds them in place and protects you from the razor-sharp points! Now I knew I was never going to fall out of a tree, but if by some chance that unlikely event were to occur, I had the perfect plan in place. That plan was, on the way down, to throw my bow as far away from me as I could so I didn't land on my arrows. Safety first! Hunting and hunting safety have come a long way since those days. Now acts like those would be looked on as crazy, but that's where the sport was for us at that time.

I continued to hunt with my bow and gun through most of high school. I was finally able to upgrade my gun from the old 20-gauge to a Remington 30.06! It didn't have a scope, but I was still able to harvest deer on a regular basis with it. I killed my first buck, a six point, with that gun too. I was so excited to finally have a rack for my wall. Papa made me a beautiful plaque for it to hang on the wall. It was made of oak and stained a dark-walnut color. John Royer did taxidermy work on the side, and he got the rack covered with a nice piece of tan leather and secured it to the plaque with a couple of screws and put a bracket on the back to hang it with. That rack and plaque still hang in my house to this day! There will only ever be one first buck for any hunter, and they are special.

CHAPTER 3

As I mentioned earlier, my parents got divorced when I was very young. The summer of 1974, when I was twelve, my dad, who lives in Montana, made plans for Karen, Bonnie, and me to come to spend some time with him and the rest of the Bergman clan for a month. I only remember seeing my dad maybe three times as a kid, and now we were going to be living with him for a month. I was really excited about the trip because we were going to fly out there, and that was going to be a first for the three of us. We would be flying out of Pittsburgh to Missoula where he would pick us up. I called the window seat for the flight on the way out, and Bonnie called it for the trip home. Karen really didn't show any interest in sitting there, which was fine with us.

Mom got us to the airport, and we were escorted to the gate. Once we were on the plane, I wasn't sure what to expect, but I was up for whatever that might be. I remember the plane after it taxied out and made that turn onto the runway, the sound of those engines revving up, and the brakes cutting loose. As the jet roared down the runway picking up speed, I was filled with excitement, mixed with a little bit of sheer terror! As the plane lifted off the ground up into the air, it was just amazing!

On the flight out, I was thinking about what it was going to be like staying with a bunch of people we really didn't know but who were also our family. I really didn't know if I was going to like it or not or if I would get homesick and want to go home. I will say it was awkward at first, but we were so busy doing things that we never had before that the time flew by. We were given freedoms and responsibilities that we had never had before. I helped my cousins bail hay! That was some hard work throwing bails up on the trailer and stacking them. The upside was we took turns driving the pickup that pulled the trailer, and I was down with that. I didn't get to drive much at home being twelve years old. I also helped my stepbrother Don move irrigation pipes. They had to be moved twice a day, and he got paid by the section. We also went to the drive-in movies as a family, but we also went just us kids. That was a cool time, having never done that before.

One night when we were there, Karen met her future husband! It must have been love at first sight, or maybe she was just awestruck by the way he ran through the concession stand while dragging a full string of two hundred firecrackers, popping and banging as he made his way through. I believe that really sealed the deal for her, but only she knows for sure. They stayed in touch after we returned home, and when Karen graduated high school, she packed up and moved to Montana. They moved in together, and when I was a senior in high school, they got married in a small church up in the Ninemile Valley in Montana. They came home after the wedding to visit and so everyone could meet Martin.

When they were home, I didn't get to spend much time with them because I was working every day. I was building swimming pools for a pool company that my friend's family owned. Since we didn't get much time together, Karen offered for me to come out to Montana and visit after the season was over and spend some time then. That sounded good to me, so I saved up my money for the rest of the summer, and sometime after Christmas, I bought a ticket on a Greyhound bound for Missoula, Montana.

Not sure who has ever traveled by bus before, but that was a long ride! The bus got off at almost every exit on the interstate and would travel five or ten miles off the interstate, stop, pick up, and drop off riders, then head back to the interstate, get back on and go to the next little town along the way. I can tell you there are a lot, and I mean a lot, of little towns between DuBois, Pennsylvania, and Missoula, Montana. I met a couple of guys from Oregon, and we hit it off. We hung out the rest of the way to Missoula where after only

11

four short days, I got off. Martin picked me up at the bus station in the middle of the night. We drove out to their house, which at the time was a little log cabin that he had built himself. The cabin was a one-room cabin with a half loft. Martin had cut the trees, skinned them, and built the cabin log by log. The cabin was cool, and the fact they built it themselves made it a bit cooler. When it got light out, Montana's full beauty was presented to me again. It was like seeing an old friend you have fond memories of that you haven't seen in a while. The country is beautiful, the people are awesome, and the adventures are endless.

My ticket's return date was one month after I departed from DuBois. After talking it over with Karen and Martin, I decided that I was going to look for a job and stay for good. I found a job and called my mom. I told her my plan and asked her to send the rest of my stuff out, and just like that, I was a resident of Montana.

The job I landed was at K-Mart working the garden patio where I proved myself and was rewarded with a full-time position running the toy department. I like to call it the "day care" department. Not my favorite job, but I was making money. I stayed with Karen and Martin a long time, until they "helped" me find a place I could afford. It was an apartment on Saulter Lane. They had lived there when Karen first moved out to Montana. My place was the bottom half of a structure, and I say it like that because I really have no idea what it was before it was apartments, but the price was right, $150 a month, everything included except for food. It fit my budget.

Being an outdoors type of person, when I say I took full advantage of what Montana had to offer, I mean it! Hunting, fishing, hiking, skiing, camping, snowmobiling, hot springing, mountain climbing, everything and anything if it had to do with the outdoors, I couldn't get enough! Hunting for me was special though. Anytime you're in the mountains, the sights, the smells, the adventure are worth the effort. I absolutely love the thought of when you're in the mountains that when you put your foot down on the ground, that you may be the first person to have ever set foot in that spot, and lots of times you are probably right. Then there are times you think that thought and look down and see a spent casing or some trash that lets you know you're not. Nevertheless, every trip out into God's creation is special in its own way.

I grew up deer hunting and love it. Montana has all kinds of deer and deer family members, like deer, mule deer, elk, moose. I find elk to be, at least in my opinion, the most regal of them all, beautiful, powerful beasts that will push you to your physical and mental limits at times. I didn't have a lot of extra cash but was saving up what I could to buy myself a hunting bow. I ended up buying a recurve bow that had a draw weight of sixty pounds at twenty-eight inches of draw. I pulled right around thirty inches, so it was about sixty-four pounds of pull to hit full draw, plenty enough power to hunt anything. I hunted hard with that bow trying to kill an elk, but it never happened for whatever reason. I did harvest plenty of game with it over the years, just never the elk.

As the early '80s unfolded, the economy was unstable. Every time I got a decent job, it would fall apart. The companies would fold, or they would relocate the business with the offer if you were willing to relocate, you could keep your job. I was working for a bakery that was relocating to Billings, and I could have gone there but didn't want to move where I didn't know anyone. I decided that I needed to learn something, anything, some kind of skill that I could live anywhere and be able to support myself. I called my mom to see if it would be okay to move home to attend school at a tech school nearby. My mom always said, "The door's always open." That was that. I moved back to DuBois at the age of twenty-four and started school. After moving back home, I missed Montana all the time.

CHAPTER 4

I went to tech school enrolled in their construction trades program. Yes, like Jesus, I would be a carpenter. It was a two-year school program, and time went by fast. I went to school from 8:00 a.m. till 2:30 p.m. Then I would work at a local supermarket from four till ten, go home, do my schoolwork or study till I was done, then get whatever sleep I could and do it all again the next day. It was hard work. I told my daughters to "work hard while you're young and strong so you don't have to when you're old." The other part of that is "Don't be a meathead with your money. Use what you need to live today, but save for tomorrow too."

I got my degree and graduated with honors, which I was proud of myself given the workload. I got a job building houses for a couple of guys I knew from around my neighborhood. I loved it. What I didn't love was wintertime in Pennsylvania. Work would slow down from little to none, which made it tough to make ends meet. Fortunately for me, the director of the school I attended liked me and offered me the chance to do a complete gut and remodel of the school office and administrative areas. I accepted, of course. That job got me through the winter while still operating in the black. I got it done a little earlier than expected, which gave me a little time to relax before the weather broke for good, and I got back to swinging the hammer full time again.

I worked all summer, and as fall approached, the director of the school contacted me again, with a different offer this time. He asked me if I would be interested in teaching at the school from October till March. I jumped at the offer. I would work from eight till two thirty, Monday through Friday, making solid money. This would once again get me through the winter with my head above water. I would be teaching exterior finish and related trades to the graduating class. Exterior finish included roofing, soffit and fascia, siding, door and window installation. Related trades included basic electric, plumbing, and use of a cutting torch. How blessed was I to be getting what I needed right when I needed it again. I did this work schedule for two years, and it was working out, but I was really looking for something that was more secure and reliable. That summer, I built houses, and while doing a job, a guy I know asked me if I wanted some extra money working on a big job doing erosion control on some hillsides and ponds. I said, "Sure."

The job was in Clearfield, a town about the size of DuBois some twenty to twenty-five miles east of DuBois. There was a giant warehouse going in over there, 1.1 million square feet to be exact, for the world's largest retailer. While I was working over there, I picked up an application for the place because I was hearing good things about the company, good pay and solid benefits and a chance for advancement. I figured, what could it hurt to apply, so I filled out the application for a general warehouse job and submitted it.

Time went by, it was late August now, and fall was approaching. I got a call from the tech school director again, which I was expecting. What I wasn't expecting was he was offering me a full-time teaching position at the school. At this same time, the warehouse called and wanted to interview me. I told the director to let me think about it, and I would let him know. I wanted to go to the interview and see what they were all about. I went and did the interview two days later after working all day. I wasn't dressed up like some there, but I felt the interview had gone well and liked what I heard about the opportunities they presented for those who wanted to advance. They told me they would be getting back to me to let me know one way or another about the job. They called me a few days later and offered me a full-time job.

I was stunned at my great fortune to have two great options before me, and I needed to decide. The job at the school was quite a bit more money but not as good in the benefits area. The warehouse job, even though less money, had solid benefits and a great chance for advancement because it was a rapidly growing company, with a chance to make more money down the road. I made my decision and made a call I wasn't looking forward to. I called the director of the school. He was excited to hear from me. I told him how much I appreciated all of the opportunities he had presented me with over the last two years and his confidence in me to do the job and be part of the full-time staff but was going to have to pass on the offer. The phone was silent for a very uncomfortable minute. He asked me how much I was going to be making, and I told him. He was shocked at my decision based on how much less the pay was. I told him that I felt that down the road, it would pay off and work out better with all of the growth. I felt like he felt I had betrayed him. I just felt the other job held more for me and was in line with what I wanted for myself and where I saw myself in the future. I can say after twenty-eight years with the choice I made, I made the right choice. I have advanced three times with the company coming up through the ranks, have a very comfortable life, and the best part of all to come from my decision is, I met my wife Megan.

We have two daughters, both are in their twenties now. Megan and the girls have been the single greatest thing to happen in my life. I have told them on more than one occasion that they saved me from me. I know if I didn't have them in my life, I wouldn't be where I am today. We are all a work in progress till the day we die. Being married with children is a lot of work. It is give and take, but if you put in the work, it is well worth the effort. We have relocated four times over the years from Pennsylvania to Michigan, then back again, then from Michigan to Ohio now. During our second run in Michigan, I was really wanting to go to Montana to go elk hunting again. Killing an elk with my bow is on my bucket list, and I'm not getting any younger, so I said something to Megan about it, and she said she didn't care if I went.

The mountains will humble you in short order if you're not prepared for the physicality of it. I thought I would use an outfitter to hunt with since I didn't live out there anymore and wasn't sure where the elk would be. I went to the hunting expo in Lansing, Michigan, in February and met a couple of guys who were outfitters who did elk hunting. We talked for a while, and they were solid straight shooting guys who sold me on their operation. I booked an early September hunt with them and told them I would show up in shape and ready to go when I got there. I decided that I would buy a compound bow for the hunt to give me more range and better penetration. As much as I wanted to get one with the recurve, I would hate myself for spending that kind of money and have a bull come in out of my effective range with that bow and have to pass the shot.

CHAPTER 5

I bought a really good bow for a really good price brand-new. I committed myself to shooting a minimum of fifty arrows a day to get intimate with the bow so I knew how it would perform in the moment of truth. I stuck to the commitment of fifty a day; some were more, some a lot more, but I put in the time. I have a belief when it comes to practicing with your bow, the only shot that counts is the very first shot. All of the shots after that are for fun and the repetition.

Here's why. When you are in a hunting situation, you are only going to get the one shot, more times than not, so the focus on doing everything right the first time is a must to be successful on a regular basis. The practice over and over again builds that muscle memory and a checklist so when you get your chance you go into autopilot, you focus on the task at hand. For my conditioning, I rode my bike. I believe riding a bike and hiking uphill in the mountains directly relate. I can tell you this. I would much rather hike uphill than downhill anytime. Going downhill is hard on your knees and feet, especially your toes, and going up or downhill in Montana is a long way. I'll take burning muscles in my thighs and claves over sore knees and my toes jammed into the toe of my boots every time. I would ride twenty miles a few times a week with the goal being to finish in as close to an hour as possible. Every now and again, I would do thirty or thirty-five miles just for the extra work for those hard days that will come in the hills. Rainy days I would ride the stationary bike in the house and lift weights. The summer passed by in no time, and it was time to go.

I flew from Detroit to Missoula with a short layover in Minneapolis. Once there, I got a rental car to drive to my buddy Chuck's place. Chuck is an old friend who still lives out there. My plan was to drive to his house to spend the night, then drive to the outfitters camp the next day. I hadn't seen Chuck in years, too many years to be exact. It was great to see him. One of life's little gifts we get to enjoy is when we go years without seeing someone, and then when we get to spend time with them, we find out nothing has changed. It's like you just saw each other yesterday. That's the way it was with us! We met in 1982, Chuck came to where I worked looking for my roommate Dave. They had grown up together. Chuck had just rolled into town after a fifty-two-hour motorcycle ride from Florida to Montana. I told him I was getting off work, and he could come over to the apartment and hang out, and that was it, we have been friends ever since. We made plans for me to return to Chuck's place after the hunt was over to hang out for a day or two, to do some fishing or upland bird hunting.

I arrived at camp the next day in midafternoon. The drive was about three hours from Chuck's place. When I got there, some of the other hunters were already there by the time I rolled in. We all would be the first hunters in camp as the season was opening the next day. The outfitters and guides all came to camp later that afternoon for dinner and a meeting afterward. The meals served at camp, which were breakfast and dinner, were excellent! One of the owners' wives did the cooking for dinner, and she could put on a meal. Breakfast was cooked by the two owners and was plenty to get the furnace burning for the uphill hike in the mornings. We all packed our own lunches every day, usually two sandwiches, chips, cookies, and plenty of water. Sometimes there was dessert leftover from dinner available to pack too. After dinner, we all went outside where we talked about several things. We also got paired up with our guide at that time. I got Tadd. He was young, about nineteen, fit and lean. The guides would come to the main lodge every morning for breakfast and pack their lunch, then we would head out to wherever we were going for the day.

Tadd and I got along well considering our age difference. We would talk on the drive, and when we got there and got out of the truck, it was funny. I would be taking my coat and hat off, rolling up my sleeves, and Tadd would be putting on a hoodie, coat, hat, and gloves for the hike uphill, two totally different body types that reacted to the morning cold in completely different ways. It would be in the low thirties in the morning. When I get to hiking, I build up a lot of heat. Tadd didn't have any fat on him, so even moving, he was chilled.

On the way up the mountain the first day, we hit a switchback. That is a place the trail turns almost 180 degrees from the direction you were heading uphill and continues the other direction uphill. I told Tadd I wanted to stop. He asked if everything was okay. I said yeah, I just want to take a minute to check out the stars. When you elk hunt, you get up early, 2:00 a.m. everyday. The plan is you start low and hope to fall in behind the elk heading uphill to bed for the day. In doing that, the thermal currents are coming downhill at that time of the day, so it puts the wind in your favor, and the elk can't smell you. You can fool an elk's eyes and their ears, but you ain't gonna fool their nose. Back to wanting to stop for a minute. I don't care where you live; on a clear night, the stars are awesome. On a clear night in Montana, the stars are just a little bit more awesome because you're just a bit closer to them. The view from that outcrop of rock was spectacular that morning. It was clear as a bell and well worth the few minutes we stood there. God's work is awesome and perfect every time.

Tadd was calling as we made our way up the ridge. Day was starting to break, and Tadd called again. We were close to where we wanted to start the day when a bull bugled back not too far off. It was so cool to hear a bull again. The smile on my face was as big as it could be. We got set up and called back and forth with the bull. The bull bugled quite a bit but fell silent, and we stayed set up for about half an hour in case the bull was coming in quiet, but he wasn't, and that was the end of that encounter for whatever reason. We moved up onto an old logging road and headed to the right at a slow pace. We were seeing elk sign, so there was no need to go storming down the road and possibly blowing them out of there. We slowly made our way around the mountain and could hear a good bull below and out ahead of us. He sounded like a good bull. He was a growler when he bugled. That doesn't mean it's a mature bull for sure, but a lot of the time, it is. As we worked our way closer, we could hear he had cow elk with him. The elk were tucked into a small canyon below us, and we were dropping down to their level and moving in on them. We must have been putting on a good stalk because we moved in right on top of a very solid mule deer buck. The buck was in my effective range, and Tadd asked if I wanted to shoot him, but with the bull still bugling, I told Tadd I would rather pass and go after the bull. We let the buck move off and continued our stalk. The mountain winds can be fickle, and as we moved to within a couple of hundred yards of the elk, the wind betrayed us, and the bull shut down.

As they say, that was that. Tadd and I hunted for the week, saw lots of great country and got lots of exercise, heard and saw some more elk, but when the week was over, I hadn't filled my tag. I look at going on a hunt as an adventure vacation with a chance to take an elk. If you base your trip's success solely on the taking of an elk, more times than not, you'll be disappointed. I had a great time, met some great people, enjoyed God's glory, and hey, there is always next year, right? I made plans to return, and I did for the next two years. I never did get an elk with them; no fault of theirs. It just didn't work out, but hey, that's hunting. The last year was tough. The wolf had been reintroduced into the region, and what an impact they made! We only heard a couple of bugles the entire week. I believe by the end of bow season, they had only taken one bull elk, which tells a story of how destructive the wolf is on ungulate populations. The other times I hunted with them, it's fair to say they averaged about two bulls harvested a week; sometimes more, sometimes less, based on the hunters' shooting accuracy. That is a great average compared to the state average of a 20 percent success rate for bowhunting elk.

The reduction of the elk population got me thinking. I should just go DIY the next year and save the money. I could go to my old spots and see if there are still elk in those areas. One day, I was talking to my nephew Andrew. He is Karen's son. He said, "Why don't you just come out and go hunting with me? I can get you one." Andrew has lived in Montana his whole life and has hunted all over the state as well as other northwestern states and Alaska. I thought, *What have I got to lose?* So we made plans to hunt the next year. We had some encounters the next year, saw some great country and got lots of exercise, but I returned home yet again with no elk. I was beginning to think, *Will this ever happen?* I made plans again to hunt with Andrew the next year!

CHAPTER 6

That year, Preslie was playing soccer in high school, Payten was playing travel softball, so the spring and summer flew by. I spent what time I could, when I could shooting, riding, and getting in the best shape I could for the upcoming hunt. One thing I learned the first time I hunted with Andrew was that he's a beast in the mountains! He would be walking through the woods with his backpack on, his bow in one hand, his cell phone in the other hand texting, and I was having one heck of a time keeping up with him! With the busy schedule, the summer flew by, and before I knew, it was time to go again.

I flew into Missoula and got there at 11:00 p.m. Andrew picked me up, and on the way back to his place, there was a giant herd of elk in a field not too far from his place. We slowed down to look at them. There were some nice bulls in the herd, which was about eighty or so head of elk.

When we got to his place, we made the game plan for the next day. The plan was to sleep in, then head to Missoula for supplies for the week, then get back to the house in time for an afternoon hunt close to Andrew's place. After the hunt, we would go back to his place, pack everything up and get ready, so in the morning, we could head out to where we would be spending the week hunting.

The next morning, on the way to town, we met my dad at the local eatery for breakfast. I made plans to see him every year I had gone out there hunting, but the visit was based on my success, and with no success, I really hadn't seen him very much. Breakfast was good. Dad paid, and we thanked him, and before we headed out, he asked, "Could we get together later in the week?"

I told him, "Sure, as soon as I get my elk."

We laughed, then Andrew and I headed into Missoula. We got what we needed and headed back out to the house. By now it was early afternoon. In Montana, the fourth largest state in the country, just running into town is a small day trip! Missoula is about thirty miles away, and boy has it grown since I lived there. The traffic there has increased so much. It is more than the infrastructure can handle, and the traffic was crazy.

When we got back to the house, we got our gear ready, which for me was taking everything out of my pack except for the bare essentials which included a knife, headlamp for the hike out in the dark, a fresh shirt, my calls, and my water bladder. It was in the mid 80's, and I sweat like crazy, so I wanted a dry shirt to put on once we reached the top of the ridge. We were going to hunt a ridge that Andrew's grandpa and I hunted all those years ago when I was nineteen. Andrew said there was still elk up there. One day after returning home from work, Ray suggested we should go up on the ridge and hunt before it got dark. So we headed out. On that hunt, both of us shot spike bulls. That hunt took place in gun season. I was so excited to harvest my first elk and was in awe at the size of it. I love deer meat, and I can tell you elk is even better table fare than deer meat. I was overjoyed that I had so much to eat!

It never seems to matter how much I prepare for the hills; it always takes a day or two to get used to the thin air. After those couple of days, I'm good to go. We had parked the truck, and like God's will, it was all uphill from there. I'm not gonna lie to you; I was sucking some air heading up the side of that ridge. When we got to the top, I changed my shirt, put on some face paint to camo out better. The wind was perfect, right in our face. We sat and listened for a bit and cooled down. Not hearing anything, we slowly worked our way to the other side of the ridge to call down over the side of it. When we reached the spot Andrew wanted to call from, he gave one cow call. We listened, then way off, we heard a bull bugle back. We continued to listen and then heard another bull much closer, maybe three hundred to four hundred yards from us. I was amazed the elk were still there. We sat down and were just enjoying the day and each other's company. Several minutes had passed since we had heard the bugle.

I said, "Maybe we should get set up a little better in case one is coming in silent."

Andrew agreed. As I rocked forward to get up—we had been sitting on our butts on the ground, and I was starting to get to my feet—when Andrew grabbed the back of my shirt and pulled me back down to the ground and said, "He's right there!"

The bull was moving from our left to our right, just off the crest of the ridge. All we could see was his rack moving along the ridgeline. I was lying flat on my back, and Andrew was still sitting on his butt on the ground. I got an arrow out of my quiver and knocked it on my string, then hooked my release on the string. I looked to see where the bull was. He was to our right and was turning to come up on to the top of the ridge to get a look around at the situation. I could see a giant ponderosa pine that he was going to pass behind on his way up onto the ridge.

I told Andrew, "When he goes behind that tree, I'm going to stand up and draw my bow."

I had my doubts about how my plan was going to play out. Trying to go from lying flat on your back to standing at full draw in one move was a lot to do without spooking the bull, but I had to try. The bull was coming up over the crest, and as soon as his head went behind the tree, I lifted my legs high and threw them forward while rocking my upper body forward. It felt like I floated to my feet and was a full draw before his head cleared the tree. The bull cleared the tree completely with his entire body and stopped perfectly broadside on top of the ridge. I was having a moment of buck fever like the fourteen-year-old kid that was sitting on that stump in doe season. Then all of the practice and preparation took over. I made sure I had hit my anchor point, acquired my peep sight, had my nose on the string and was figuring he was forty yards out.

I asked Andrew, "How far?"

He said, "Give me a second."

I could hear him working the button on his rangefinder over and over.

I asked again, "How far?"

Andrew said, "I can only see his rack and can't get a range off of it."

He was still on the ground and had a totally different view of the situation than I did. At this time, I had been at full draw for about forty-five seconds, and the bull was starting to look like he had better places to be. I felt good with my estimate of forty yards and had settled on that for my shot. Andrew was still clicking away when the bull lifted his head, and I heard him say, "Thirty-eight yards."

As soon as he said that, I squeezed the trigger, and the arrow was on its way. The flight was true, and the arrow buried right behind the bull's shoulder about a third of the way up his chest.

I looked at Andrew and said, "I smoked him!"

Andrew said, "It sounded good."

And I repeated, "I smoked him!"

Upon impact, the bull spun around and took off down over the hill out of sight. I was in disbelief! Six years of trying, working out, shooting my bow, riding my bike mile after mile—everything I had done to try to make this happen all just came together. Andrew was up on his feet. I gave him as big a hug as I could because he was squeezing me pretty hard too. We both told each other "good job." I couldn't stop smiling! That lasted for days after by the way. Andrew went and found my arrow. It had passed through the elk completely, and he found it sticking in a tree twenty yards on the other side of where the elk had been standing during the shot.

I have a friend in Michigan. I call him Dirsch, which is short for his last name. We lived about a mile from each other. He was familiar with my struggle to take an elk with the bow. I sent him a picture of my arrow through text. Dirsch texted right back asking if I bagged. I thought the ear-to-ear smile would have given it away, but I still sent back a yes! Six years and fifteen minutes to accomplish a bucket list goal that really had started thirty-one years ago. I hadn't even been in Montana for twenty-four hours when I got my bull. After everything it took for me to get it done, I could understand Dirsch asking me the question about bagging, knowing the struggle and the fact he knew I just left the evening before.

Andrew and I started down over the side of the ridge, and we split apart about thirty to forty yards when I heard him yell, "I found him."

What a relief. I knew in my mind he had to be done, but until I heard that, there was still a bit of doubt. The bull had gone about seventy-five yards before piling up on the hillside. We took a bunch of photos, then the work started. We were both skinning the bull out and quartering him up for the pack out. The bull was a five-by-five bull, not the biggest bull in the world but the biggest one I had ever killed. He looked like he would be pushing the world record when he broke the ridge right before I shot. We worked on him for about an hour before we had him quartered up and packed up. It would be about a mile pack, which isn't really that far, but we were going to bring the whole thing out in one trip. While we were sitting there before we headed out, Andrew picked up movement below us on the hillside. It was a wolf. He must have smelled the kill. As soon as he realized something wasn't quite right, he disappeared like a vapor into the growing darkness, a brief but very cool encounter for sure.

As I said before, we had skinned and boned out the elk. Both of our packs were packed full of meat, and what didn't fit in them we tied to the outside of them. I have no idea what my pack weighed, but after I slid up to it on the hillside sitting on my butt and got the shoulder straps over my shoulders, Andrew had to help get me up off the ground. On top of that, there was the head and cape to carry. The bull was a decent five-by-5 bull. I was going to get the head mounted after the saga it had been for me to get one. He was a true trophy to me. Andrew helped me with the head too as we took turns carrying it. We were coming out heavy for sure because we were doing it in one trip, but I loved every minute of it. Not sure why I had pulled all of my gear out of my pack before we went, but I was glad I had because I needed all the space. We got back to the truck, loaded everything up, and headed back to the house.

I called Megan and told her about the hunt and how short and how easy it had seemed after going through so much up to that point to get one. I had sent her a picture that Andrew took of me with the bull.

Megan sent back,

Wow that's a big sucker!

Megan was happy for me and as much in disbelief as I was that it had happened so fast on the first day. She has always been so supportive of me in my quest to accomplish this. There aren't enough words to tell her how much I appreciate all the sacrifices she made for me to be able to do this.

We got back to the house and unpacked everything. We laid some tarps out on the garage floor and spread out the meat on them to cool it down. We grabbed a couple of cold beverages and got busy. Andrew was caping out the head, and I was breaking down the quarters into smaller chunks to help it cool down faster. While we were busy, I was thinking to myself, *That was so easy. How could this have taken so long to accomplish? Oh yeah, and today's date, Friday the thirteenth!* Andrew still had his bull tag and we had the rest of the week to hunt and we did. We hunted a few different spots, had some cool encounters, and saw some awesome country, but it didn't work out for him. Andrew, since he lives out there, wouldn't shoot a bull the size of the one I got. He's always looking for something bigger. I guess when you live there you can do that. Time was up, and the hunt was over. It was time to go home.

CHAPTER 7

I had mentioned my buddy Dirsch. He and I met through work. He was hired to work in my department at the warehouse when we moved to Michigan. He was eighteen or nineteen I guess at that time. Getting to know him through work, we found we had mutual interests like hunting and fishing, and through those interests, our friendship grew. When we moved back to Pennsylvania after our first stay in Michigan, Dirsch had come to Pennsylvania to give some mountain hunting a try, and I was still going back to Michigan every year to hunt too. Eventually, we ended up moving back to Michigan and bought a great place a mile away from where Dirsch and his wife Courtney lived. It was a beautiful house that sat on twenty acres of land, just off of a creek bottom, and the woods I owned were surrounded by corn and soybean fields. I had great deer, turkey, and rabbit hunting on my place, and you could find morel mushrooms here and there on the place.

After I got home, Dirsch and I got together and talked more in-depth about the trip. Dirsch told me he would like to go with me, if I didn't mind. I told him I would talk with Andrew and see if he was good with it and let him know. Andrew said he was fine with Dirsch coming. I told Dirsch that we would need to apply in the spring for our licenses, which we did. We found out in May that we had indeed been successful in securing tags. Now that we had tags, we knew we could start to make some solid plans for the trip. Andrew and his buddy Cam, who both have horses, were making some trips deep into the backcountry scouting for elk. They had found a sweet spot ten miles back into the mountains that they settled on for the hunt.

They had seen several good bulls back in there and heard even more. The area held many mountain lakes that should be good fishing for us while we were in there. Dirsch and I were excited to get the chance to do a hunt like they did in the old days with a pack train of horses deep in the remote mountains. We would have a wall tent to sleep in, and because we were taking horses in, we would be much more comfortable because we could take so much more with us than you can carry in just your backpack.

Dirsch bought a bike, and we were riding quite a bit, shooting daily, either together or by ourselves. We were both in good shape and shooting well as the summer rolled into September, and just like that, it was time to go. Our flight was getting in late, 11:00 p.m. Andrew picked us up at the airport, and we headed to his place. Andrew had relocated that year to a place just outside of Frenchtown in the prairie land to the west of town. The place was kind of an aboveground underground house. It was built aboveground but had earth piled up around it to help insulate it to keep it cool in the summer and warmer in the winter. It was a pretty cool place. We settled in for the night.

The next morning, Dirsch and I got up and shot our bows to make sure they were good to go after the treatment baggage tends to get from the airlines, and the change in altitude can affect your bow too. Your bow, if it is off due to altitude, will usually shoot higher than at the altitude you live at, if that is lower, due to the thin air. The bows were good; just a bit high but nothing that needed to be adjusted. The anticipation was building as it always does as we were busy getting the gear ready. I always feel a bit like a kid on Christmas eve, filled with all of the excitement of not knowing what was to come.

Getting ready to go into the mountains on foot versus going on horseback is way easier. The amount of stuff you take to be more comfortable, along with the horse tackle and what you need to care for the horses properly is a lot. We got that ready, then headed to Missoula to get supplies. After two full carts of food, drinks, and ice, we got fueled up and headed for the trailhead. The trailhead was about a two-hour drive. When we got there, Cam was already there.

He had stuff everywhere. It looked like a barn had blown up! There were horses, hay, saddles, pack saddles, bridles, panyards (which are where you put all the stuff in for the horses to haul), camping gear, food, water, rope, tarps. It was a big ordeal or at least looked like one. When you are packing up the panyards you need to balance out the weight for the horses to keep their balance, so we were busy splitting the gear up into the panyards and trying to get them as close to the same weights for a balanced load. Andrew and Cam knew how much each horse could handle, and Cam had a scale he brought to get an actual weight. They were really good at getting the loads close right off the bat. We had to make a few slight adjustments in the panyards, but they were really close from the start. Andrew and Cam's knowledge of the pack string process, tying knots, tying the horses off to each other, loading the horses, was impressive.

Now Dirsch and I are not very horse savvy! Thank God, both of them had some easy to ride horses for dummies, and guess who got to ride them? The day was clear, and you could tell it was going to get hot. Montana is hot and dry. You feel the warmth, but you don't build up much sweat. It just dries right up, so you can dehydrate quickly. Dirsch and I were mounted up, without incident I might add, and we each had on our backpacks with our bows secured in them and our water bladders filled to the top for the ride and our guns holstered on our sides. The area we were going had grizzlies in it. We also had pepper spray as a first line of defense in the rare event something should happen and the guns as a last line of defense.

I want to share with you one of the major differences of hiking versus riding horses into the mountains. You're not running yourself into the ground on the way in, so when you get to camp, you're not beat, with a bunch of work to do once you get there. The second thing is time was flying by because of the novelty of riding the horses. When you ride, you have time to look around and enjoy the beauty of your surroundings. Wild game, when you're walking, will see you and bust out of there, but when you're sitting on a horse, they'll stand there and look at you like, *What in the world is that?* The third thing I learned was when you're on horseback you can relax and have some nice wine to enjoy on your trip into the rugged mountains! Not

31

something I'd ever done on foot. We were having a blast, and as we continued to snake our way toward camp, the daylight was fading over the last ridge to the west.

We were now right above camp and needed to navigate a substantial rockslide downhill to camp on horseback. It was getting darker, and we put on our headlamps. Cam said to turn on the red lamp because it was hard for the horses to see with the white light blinding them, so we turned on the red lamp and headed downhill. Quite the sound hearing a packtrain of horses clacking their way through a rockslide. I'm not going to lie; I was a bit nervous, but the horses were great. They didn't slip a bit, and we made camp as it was getting to be completely dark out.

CHAPTER 8

The guys had been in there the week before and set up the wall tent, so that was done. We unloaded the horses and tethered them off in a nice green grassy area for the night. We got our sleeping bags and air mattresses set up in the tent, then got a bite to eat, enjoyed a cold beer or two, and talked about the next day's plan.

Cam and Andrew would be riding back out in the morning to get more hay for the horses and some more supplies, then would ride back into camp. Dirsch and I were going hunting! He and I were getting our backpacks loaded up with what we were going to need and the rest of our gear ready for the day. The excitement meters were buried in the red, and it was hard to leave the fireside and go to bed when we had all of our stuff ready.

Even though we had a wall tent, it was tight with four grown men in there with all of our stuff. I know I snore, but I also know I wasn't the only one in there who was snoring that night. I was by the door, so if anyone had to get out for a nature call, it woke everyone up I think, but me for sure.

Morning broke dark and chilly. We got up and got moving, had the usual breakfast of oatmeal and coffee. We made some sandwiches and headed up the ridge to the top. Cam and Andrew headed out on the horses to go into town. We said we would see them back at camp around dark. Our plan was to make the ridge top and wait there until it was light out and listen for elk. The top of that ridge was the perfect spot to listen. You could see and hear down into three different drainages.

One of the things I love about being in the mountains is watching the sun come up over the mountains and listening to the wild world wake up to a new day. It's in moments like that you know there has got to be a God, to be able to witness such a sight. We could see two lakes; one below us to the north, the other southeast. We decided to work our way toward the one to the southeast, only because it looked like an easier hike. We hadn't heard any elk from the ridge, but there was plenty of signs they were around. We were high on life being in such an awesome place. We worked our way to the lake, and when we broke out of the timber, we found ourselves on top of a huge rock cut that ran to the right and dropped off right into the lake and continued out of sight down into the depths of the crystal-clear lake, and that cut was screaming at me, *Get out your fishing rod and cast out along the cut!*

I dropped my pack and was getting my rod out and set up. I keep a fishing rod and reel at Chuck's place, so every time I go to Montana, I have a fishing rod I can use. We had stopped by and got my rod on the way to the trailhead and grabbed one for Dirsch too. I was set up and looked at Dirsch. He was standing there looking at me getting ready.

I said, "Where's your rod?"

He said, "I left it at camp."

I shook my head and threw my Panther Martin as far out into the lake as I could along the cut and let it sink a bit, then started the slow roll back along the cut. It took all of about five cranks on the reel, and bam, "Fish on!"

Same thing happened the second cast and the third. Well you get it; it was fish on every cast! I asked Dirsch if he wanted to give it a go, and oddly enough, he did. I handed him my rod, and on his first cast, it was fish on. We took turns catching fish, and we caught a lot.

One that we returned to the lake wasn't doing well after the fight, and we got it back out of the water. We built a fire right there on the rock cut and cooked the trout over the fire on a stick and ate it just like that, no seasonings other than smoke from the fire. It was fantastic! After that, we got back to the hunt. There was a shallow draw that ran uphill from the lake to the north and to a ridge that I wanted to get on and hike, so we headed in that general direction.

As we were moving slowly up the draw, we caught movement in front of us on the ground. It was a flock of Franklin's grouse, and the mystical flight of the arrow ensued. Dirsch shot first and got one. Then I shot and missed, and I would like to say it was a really hard shot, but the truth was it was a cake shot, and I peeked when I pulled my trigger. Dirsch got another one, then I got one, then another. Four down for the count. It was looking like grouse is what was for dinner. We took some good photos of our bounty and continued on. We hunted hard for the rest of the day but never saw or heard any elk, so we headed back toward camp. On the way, Dirsch was able to secure one more grouse for the pot. We felt like we had enough to feed the four of us and then some. Great day in the field for sure.

When we arrived at camp, Andrew and Cam weren't there, but we figured, twenty miles on horseback, two hours to town, two hours back, they would be along soon. So we set about getting over to the running water so we could clean up our grouse. There was a seep on the hillside that Andrew had worked a hose up into the night before. It started out muddy but had cleared up and was running great, crystal clear water right out of the ground, no need to boil before drinking. Drinking water in the mountains is tricky. If you drink from a lake or a stream without a filter system or boiling the water first, you can contract a miserable little thing called giardia. If you're getting your water right out of the ground, you don't have to worry about it. Giardia is caused from animal waste in the water, which has a parasite. When you drink it, the parasite gains entry to your body and creates havoc on your digestive tract from the stomach down. It can clear up on its own, but in severe cases, you need antibiotics to get rid of it. I have never had it, but from what I hear, it is terrible.

We boned out the grouse and washed it up with the water from the hose. Dirsch was cutting up potatoes, carrots, and onions which we boiled. We sliced the grouse about a quarter inch thick and cooked the meat with onions and portobello mushrooms, with a poppy seed dressing that we would pour over the veggies. We were roughing it up there in the high lonesome. We ate with no sign of Andrew or Cam as darkness had set in. We were sitting by the fire when Dirsch said he thought he could hear them coming down the slide. My hearing is not the best, but I could hear them shortly after Dirsch said he could, then we could see their headlamps, rocking as they picked their way down through the rocks.

When they got into camp, we asked, "What took so long?"

They said, "We had some issues along the way and had a conversation with a DNR officer who said we needed to be very careful in here, and that they knew of three grizzlies in the area, two of them were big males, that should not be taken lightly."

They also found out about a rule they have in Montana that states that you can't camp for more than fourteen days in any spot. If you camp in a spot for fourteen days, you must then break camp and have to move a specific distance from that spot, which is, and don't quote me on this, but I thought it was two miles. That meant even though we had only spent one night in the tent, we would be moving in the morning because the DNR had observed the tent for the past two weekends from the air in that spot.

The guys got some food and ate. Cam was going to eat and head back out because his grandmother wasn't feeling well. I wasn't so sure that I would be too excited about going out for another ten-mile ride in the dark after logging twenty already for the day. It didn't even faze Cam though. After he ate, he mounted up and rode out of camp. We could hear the horses' shoes clacking off the rocks for a while and could see glimpses of Cam's red headlamp every once in a while, and then the sound and the light disappeared into the darkness. Andrew and Cam are both born and raised in Montana, and they are both competent, self-assured outdoorsmen who have skills and experience that bring with them a certain amount of confidence in their abilities.

Andrew has been in the mountains his whole life and has had plenty of meals in the mountains that were provided from the land while in the mountains. He said the meal we prepared was the best or second best he had ever had in the mountains. I am sure that Dirsch and I took that as a big endorsement of our efforts and skills. We sat by the fire and talked about our options of where we could relocate to in the morning. We decided to move to the lake that Dirsch and I had fished earlier that day. There was a nice flat grassy area by the lake where the horses could hangout and feed, not to mention a lake full of fish. When morning broke, we got up and got after it, tearing down the tent and putting everything back the way it was before anyone had camped there. We loaded everything up on the horses and headed up over the top of the ridge and down into the lake area. It was a drag to give up the morning hunt, but you gotta do what you gotta do.

Once we got to the lake, we got the horses set up in the grassy area. We cut a pole to tie them off too in an area where they would be in the shade in the heat of the day that had lots of lush grass for them to feed on and was close to the lake for watering. We talked about setting up the wall tent again, then decided not to. I always have a tarp in my backpack for whatever may arise, and we decided to pitch it and just sleep under it. We still had the mini cots, air pads, and sleeping bags, so it made sense and saved us some time. The forecast was favorable, and if we did get rain, we had the tarp. Given the time of day, we decided to spend more time tweaking camp, then fish and get ready for the next day's hunt. One thing we did do differently based on the info on the bears was we hauled the panyards with the food in them up over the rock cut, about one hundred yards from camp, and strung them up in the trees about fifteen to eighteen feet up.

After we got things set in camp, we grabbed the fishing rods and hit the lake. The fishing was great. We all caught several fish, and it's fair to say all of them were fourteen to eighteen inches long, and they fought hard. We were using light-action rods with a four-pound test line, which made all the fish feel like monsters and made for great fun.

We got up the next morning and hiked to the top of the ridge. We were seeing elk scat; some fresh, some not. But there was elk around for sure. We hit the top of the ridge and decided to sit down and watch the sun rise. On top of the ridge, we all had phone service, so we all sent word to our women that we were fine and that we loved and missed them. After watching the sun rise, we decided to move north. When we crested the next ridge's top, Andrew threw out a bugle and got a bull to sound off from the next ridge over. We weren't exactly sure where he was on the ridge, just what ridge the bugle had come from. The three of us climbed on top of a rock outcrop, and all of us started to cow call across the valley to the bull. He responded right back which was a good sign, but he was a long way off. He continued to bugle on his own, so I got out my binos, and while lying flat on the rock, I started glassing hard to see if I could catch a glimpse of him to see what he looked like. The bull was moving back and forth on the ridge based on his calls coming to us, which made me think he was herding cows around. Then I heard him by a pretty good size opening and was fixed on that spot. Then I saw him move through the opening and told the guys he was a good bull. I was following his movement through the binos and saw him go through another opening and turn downhill and lost sight of him. I told the guys I thought he was coming. I don't think Andrew and Dirsch thought I was serious because he was so far away, but I told them we should get set up.

The bull sounded off again, and this time he sounded farther away! I told the guys based on my turkey hunting in Pennsylvania, that a turkey on the ridge across from you, when they gobble, they sound close, but when they commit to coming in and descend down into the hollow, they sound like they have moved off when they are actually coming up the hillside to you. I shared that with the guys as the bull bugled again and sounded even farther off.

Before we had heard the bull the first time, Dirsch had a nature call and had gone off out on the ridge we were on. He did his thing and came back and joined us. The next time we heard the bull, he sounded closer, and it was clear then that he was indeed on the same ridge as us and down below us, no more than a couple of hundred yards and closing the distance fast. We scrambled to get set up. The wind was good and in our favor as the thermals had switched and were coming uphill into our faces. Andrew stayed close to where we had been calling from, and Dirsch and I moved out the ridge. Dirsch set up, and I moved about forty to fifty yards past him just in case the bull got by him, but it was his bull to kill. Andrew called, and the bull called back basically right on top of us. A few tense moments went by as I was straining to see what was going on. Then the bull barked, not good, and bolted down the ridge in the direction he had approached from.

I moved up to Dirsch and asked, "Did you get busted?"

He said, "No, he must have busted you."

I asked, "How far away was he?"

Dirsch said, "He was in range but was facing me, and I was waiting for him to turn for a better shot."

The wind was in our favor, and I couldn't see him or the bull, so I was sure he didn't bust me.

Andrew got up and came over and asked, "What happened?"

We both told our stories of the encounter, and Andrew of course said, "I could see him perfectly wide open broadside in bow range from where I was and figured Dirsch got busted trying to draw his bow." As we were standing there, Andrew asked Dirsch, "Where was he standing?"

Dirsch went to where the bull had been standing, and then it was clear why the bull had bolted. When the bull came up over the hillside, he walked to within a few feet of where Dirsch had his "call of nature"! What are the chances of that? Pretty good, I guess.

We hunted the rest of the day without any more encounters. As a matter of fact, we hunted the rest of the time there, and the only other bugle I heard was in the middle of the night in the direction of another lake below the one we were camped at. I told the guys in the morning about the bugle, and we headed in that direction for the day but had no encounters. When we got back to camp, we got unpacked and had a beer.

We had a camp bucket we took in with us. It was a bucket made of a material that would hold water. It had a plastic rim with a wire handle, and the whole thing would collapse upon itself. It took up little room, so it was a great tool to have along.

We had the bucket set up in a shady spot in our camp. It was full of water from the lake and beer. The beer was nice and cool every day when we returned from the hunt, from sitting all night when the temps would dip into the low forties and high thirties and with it sitting in a shady spot all day. The lake water was cold! We would go to the cut and jump into the lake almost every day to cool off and clean up. It would take your breath away.

One day, we talked about how cold the lake was when we jumped in and figured the water at the bottom may be even colder, so we came up with the plan to take the beer bucket to the cut and lower it to the bottom of the lake with a rock on top of the beer to keep it in the bucket so we could have crisp cold beer when we got back. The next morning, we did just that and tied the rope off to a tree that was on top of the rocks and headed out. When we got back from our hunt, I think we all had forgotten about our ice-cold prize that awaited us on the bottom of the lake. Someone walked to the old spot for a beer, and then we realized we needed to pull it up from the depths of the lake. I said I would go and get it. I headed over to the cut and grabbed the rope and started to pull it up. I think I was drooling a bit in anticipation of the first big gulp of ice-cold beer. The bucket reached the top of the water, and I pulled a bit harder since I lost the buoyancy of the water helping me lift the bucket. Never thinking about possible outcomes of pulling on the rope harder, I pulled away, and then the handle popped out of the rim of the bucket, and it all splashed back into the lake! I shouted out a profane word that rhymes with truck!

When the bucket hit the water, some of the beer sank to the bottom along with the bucket and rock. Some of the beer had come out on impact and was floating and dispersing to the four winds in the lake. I was standing there wondering why some floated and others sank. When I dropped the F bomb, the guys said, "What's going on?"

I told them, and Andrew said, "You need to get them all back out of the lake because this is a wilderness area, and you can't litter."

I thought, *Littering? Heck, we needed to get them back because we can't just run down to the corner store and get more.* Hearing that, I started to take my pants off and remembered that I had jumped in the lake and got cleaned up earlier, and when I got out, I just put my pants back on. I was going commando style after that. So now I knew I was going in, and I was going in my birthday suit and doing so with two guys more than willing to come over with their phones and video the whole thing. So I dropped my pants and bailed off the cliff into the water. When I came up, I could hear both of my buddies cracking up and getting closer. I was swimming around doing my best water cowboy I could, swimming around herding up beers with my chest and swimming them over to get them to Dirsch as he laughed and snapped photos. Once I got all the ones from the top of the water, I could see the others down there. They looked to be about twelve to fifteen feet down. The bucket and rock were only about seven or eight feet, so I got the bucket first.

I was getting pretty cold by this time and not looking forward to going deeper, but down I went again and again only to surface to the sound of my two buddies laughing uncontrollably. After I gave the last one to Dirsch, I swam over and slithered up on the sun-warmed rocks. I got my pants back on and headed back over to camp and sat by the fire to warm up. After all of that and once I had warmed up, I was all about having my crisp ice-cold beer! I grabbed one, cracked it open, took a big old gulp only to find it wasn't any colder than it was any other day when it was just sitting in the bucket in the shade! We laughed about that the rest of the day.

We did go fishing and kept five or six for dinner. Andrew had brought in some seasonings and everything else he needed to make up a recipe he really liked with trout. When we were fishing, Dirsch had caught the trip lunker, a beauty about nineteen or twenty inches long. Andrew doctored up the fish and cooked them in the fire wrapped in foil with some butter and seasonings. It was a fantastic combination and an outstanding meal, and there was plenty to go around. The trip was winding down, and Cam would be riding in to help pack everything out.

When Cam got into the lake, we figured we were one horse shy for everyone to ride out. We talked about it and decided we would take turns riding and walking. I said I would walk first. So when all of the panyards were packed and weighed, the horses loaded up, the guys said they would be heading out in a few minutes. I decided to head out then, figuring they would catch up to me somewhere along the way. I had my backpack, with a full bladder of water and my

.44 Mag on my side; that was it. I set out on foot heading uphill to get to the ridge the first leg of the ten-mile journey out. Well, they finally caught up to me when I was descending down the hill right above the trucks! I saw them coming out of a small drainage in the bottom. I had set down a couple of times and even walked off in the wrong direction for about half a mile and had to hike it back, and they hadn't caught up to me till we got to the truck? I had run out of water quite a while ago and was dehydrated. When we met up in the bottom, I asked if they had any water. All they had was some semi warm beer. I didn't care; it was wet, and I drank one down. When we got back to the trucks, someone found a bottle of water that was still pretty cold in a cooler, and I downed that too. We got everything loaded up and headed to town to get some pizza. At dinner, we talked about the next year, and all agreed to give it another go. Dirsch and I headed home a couple of days later.

CHAPTER 9

The next year, we were lucky enough to draw again. Through the year, we made and finalized plans with Andrew for the hunt. September arrived, and before you knew it, we were standing on the ground in Missoula.

During the year, Andrew had moved to Minnesota and was driving from there to Missoula with the intention he would arrive right around the time our flight landed. The timing was pretty good, and we didn't have to wait long after we landed. We got our bags, and he showed up right after that.

After Andrew picked us up, we headed into town. On the way, Andrew told us that he had applied earlier in the year for a mountain goat tag and didn't get selected, but he was on a list, so if anyone couldn't make their trip, their tag would be given to whoever was on the top of the waiting list. Well, someone had some health issue come up and wasn't going to be able to make the trip and their tag was now available. And he was lucky enough to be on the top of the list for the tag, and the tag was now his. I was happy for him to have landed the tag, at the same time, not so happy to find out that he wanted to combine his goat hunt with our elk hunt. My concern was that for Dirsch and I, there are elk at eleven thousand feet but not that many, and there aren't many goats down where there are more elk. I didn't want to spend time that high up in the rocky tops of the mountains when there were greener pastures down below. After discussion, we decided not to hunt together. Andrew and his dad, Martin, headed south to the Gallatin National Forest to hunt for his goat, and Dirsch and I would regroup and hunt for elk on some of my old hunting grounds. I'm lucky to have my old friend Chuck still living out there. I let him know our situation, and he hooked us up big time. Chuck gave us a truck, tent, totes, cooler, and a lot of other essential things we needed. We went to town to get everything else we needed and headed out. We had a few hours' drive to where I wanted to go.

When we got there, we set up camp and made our plan for the next day. We decided to hike uphill from camp on this long ridge, then we would cross a saddle to another ridge and hunt it back quite aways, then cross the drainage and back to the top of the ridge we hiked up, then back to camp. It would be a good first-day hunt to get acclimated to the altitude, see some beautiful country, and get some good exercise and, who knows, maybe an elk.

We slept well that night and in the morning, got up, ate breakfast, packed lunch, and headed out. The morning was clear and crisp as we worked our way uphill. We were not seeing much fresh sign at all. The area we were hunting, you don't hear much bugling because of the wolves. The elk don't like to draw much attention to themselves. You can definitely tell the difference when you hunt an area with wolves versus one that doesn't. Areas that do have them, the elk are pretty tight-lipped because if they do sound off, they just may be what's for dinner.

We were camped at just above six thousand feet. Our hunt took us another 1,700 feet above camp elevation. You could tell as you went the air was thin and getting thinner. When we hit the saddle, we took a break. We had been calling every now and then as we climbed higher and higher, with no responses coming back. After our break, we crossed over the saddle to the other ridge. That ridge had thicker cover than the one we followed up. The dense brush slowed our pace, but that's not a bad thing when you're hunting. As we made our way down the ridge, it was more of the same, not much sign and for sure not much fresh sign. We were concerned with the lack of elk sign for sure, and we talked about it quite a bit. We decided that we would finish out the hunt, and if nothing improved, we would hunt down from camp in the morning. In the morning, if we weren't seeing any good signs, we would decide our plan of action after that.

Montana is one place where when you hear someone say "If you don't like the weather, wait five minutes. It will change," it is true. That day, while we were out, it had started to rain and then became mixed with snow, then just turned to snow. The one thing that came from that was I knew I had a boot issue. My feet were getting wet. Not a good thing to have to deal with in an unforgiving environment. Wet feet lead to cold, wet, and sore feet. Take my word for it. You don't want sore feet when almost every step you take for a week is uphill, downhill, or side hill. It can be miserable! By the time we got back to camp, the snow was sticking to the ground, and my feet were soaked. We never heard or saw any elk on our hunt.

Dirsch had an app on his phone that tracks your travel path. It said we had taken 23,666 steps, which equaled eleven miles. Not a bad first hunt of the trip. When we got back to camp, we changed out of our wet gear and put on dry. We got a fire going and got our damp stuff hanging to dry as well as my boots.

Later on, we took a ride down the road in the truck. We hadn't brought our bows, and we ended up running into some grouse. Knowing Chuck, I told Dirsch to look under the seat or in the glove box, that Chuck most likely had his .22-caliber pistol in the truck somewhere. Sure enough, he did. We found it under the seat. Dirsch got to go first, and it took a few shots, but he got one with the pistol. We were on our way back to camp when he got his bird, and we were almost to camp when we ran into a few more. And I was able to take one for myself. Looked like grouse for dinner.

When we got back to camp, we stoked the fire back up and checked our gear to see how dry it was. The clothes were good, but my boots had a way to go. I ended up pulling my insoles out and put some rocks that had been heated by the fire inside of them to finish drying them out. It worked pretty good actually, but you need to be careful doing things like that. You could find yourself out of a pair of boots.

We decided to go old style on the grouse for dinner. We decided to cook them over the open fire on a spit. I always have seasonings in my pack in case I get into fish or grouse. We seasoned up the birds and put them to the fire. We decided, for a side dish, we would make

45

some mac and cheese. While the birds were cooking, we decided to build a bench to sit on. We cut a couple of logs about five inches in diameter and tied them together with some paracord. We stacked up two piles of stones and put the logs on top of them. It was pretty good, and after some shimming, it was really good. It was pretty comfortable and better than having a soggy bottom from sitting on what was around. I was looking forward to trying the grouse since I had never tried this method before. To quote my daughter Payten, "If I'm being honest…," it wasn't that good. The fire had dried it out, and it was tough with not much flavor. I ended up cutting mine up and putting it in with my portion of the mac and cheese. We had a couple of drinks and hit the sack.

I have camped out in Montana plenty of times, even in the dead of winter. That night was one of the coldest nights I have ever spent in the wild. It snowed some that night, and when we got up, I don't think either of us were exactly excited to get out of our sleeping bags. We got out of our bags and got dressed. We fired up the truck which we had named Big Red. Big Red was a Ford Ranger, red in color with a red topper on the bed, 4-wheel drive. Solid little ride! We hopped in Big Red to get warmed up. We had made our morning coffee and were sitting in Big Red trying to talk ourselves out of just driving to town for a nice hot breakfast of bacon and eggs. I was also thinking about my boot situation.

I said to Dirsch, "Let's at least hunt until my feet are soaked, to the point I can't take it anymore, then go to town. Maybe I can get a pair of boots in there too."

He agreed, and we got ourselves ready and headed out. We had decided to walk the road to a gated road and head downhill from there, in the hopes of running into the elk as they came up to bed. The road worked down a ridge through the timber and broke out into sagebrush that went down to the fields in the valley. The wind wasn't the best. It was all over the place, so we would need some luck if we got into them.

We got to the road and headed down the ridge. We hadn't gone far, maybe three hundred to four hundred yards, when I heard elk moving off through the trees. I motioned to stop. Right then, I could see a bull coming off the sagebrush into the timber, a raghorn. I gave a cow call, and he headed our way. I had an opening, and he was within range, but I wanted Dirsch to get one, so I held off. I had my rangefinder in my hand. We were standing in the middle of the road as the bull was moving in on us from our left to right.

I said to Dirsch, "Let me know when you have a shot."

Just then, he said, "Now."

I called, and the bull stopped. Dirsch was at full draw already, and I got a yardage and said, "Forty-five yards," and the arrow was on its way! It hit the bull in the perfect spot. The bull spun around and headed back down the ridge the way he had come in.

We looked at each other, all wide-eyed with big smiles. We gave each other a big hug. We couldn't believe our luck! My feet weren't even wet at all! We gave the bull some time and followed him up. Upon the hit, the bull went at full speed and had made it about 150 yards down the ridge. We boned out the bull, filled our packs, and started up the ridge to the road. Camp was only a quarter of a mile down the road, so when we got everything up to the road, we hiked to camp and tore it down, loaded everything into the truck and drove up to where we had dropped everything. We loaded everything up and started out for Chuck's place. Once we got there, we took care of the meat. Then we unloaded the truck and laid everything out to dry. We had stuff all over the place. After Dirsch got the elk, we were so geeked up that we never did eat breakfast! We did celebrate a bit, had a good meal and a nice hot shower, and got a good night's sleep.

The next morning, we drove to Missoula, and I got a new pair of boots. We decided to spend the day repacking all of the gear and decided the next day, we would hunt up on the hill behind Chuck's place. He has been into elk up there in the past, and you never know. Elk are like gold. They're where you find them! The next morning, it was pouring rain—I mean pouring! To say I was less than inspired to go would be a true statement. The hill behind Chuck's house was steep and covered with loose rock. Add in the rain, and it was slippery as all get out. The only good thing about any of it was it was only a few hundred yards to get on the ridge. I was soaked from sweat and rain by the time we broke the ridge top. We hiked and called

47

and hunted the biggest part of the day but only saw a muley doe. On our way back down the ridge, we did find a mountain lion track in one of our boot tracks from when we went up the ridge. Not sure if I mentioned this or not, but I hate mountain lions! They are big souped-up wildcats that are quiet, strong killing machines that hunt what we were hunting. While we are hunting elk, we call and sound like what the cats are hunting too. I'm not sure if it was a coincidence or not, but it makes you wonder if the cat was actually hunting us or if it just happened to have walked in one of our tracks sometime after we had hiked through there?

We did a few more day hunts and even went back down to where Dirsch got his bull again for a couple of days. One night when we were down there, we had fallen asleep, and sometime during the night, I heard a bull bugle right outside of camp. I don't think he could have been more than fifty yards away. He sounded off, three times. I didn't say anything to Dirsch because I figured he had heard the bull with it being so close. In the morning, I asked him about it, and he said that he must have slept right through it because he hadn't heard a thing. When we got out of the tent in the morning, we called, and the bull called back. He was below us, and we took up pursuit. The bull and his cows took us for a nice morning workout! We ended up clear down in the bottom by the fields, and they gave us the slip, so we got to hike all the way back up out of there to camp. Hey, that's elk hunting.

We didn't really have any other encounters, and the trip was winding down. I wanted to spend some time with Chuck as well as see my dad and my sisters. We headed back to Chuck's for the last couple of days. We fished the Blackfoot river with Chuck a couple of times! Chuck's son, Brian, says to people, "My dad could catch a fish in a mud puddle!" And I believe he could. He is a great fisherman! We had breakfast with my dad one morning and went to Karen's house and hung out with her. I felt good that I actually did visit some, and it always amazes me just how fast the trip comes to an end. And this one was over much too fast, and we headed home!

CHAPTER 10

Dirsch was bit with fever. He had a great time and wanted to go again. I was good with it, so we applied again and got tags again. It is always good to share the hunt with someone. We had put in for the elk combo tag. This gives you an elk tag, fishing license, upland game bird license, and your conservation license. I gave up on the big game combo license because it seemed like every time I saw a good buck, we were also into elk, and I never ended up shooting the buck. I love deer meat, but elk is much better than deer in my opinion. So why spend the money on the extra tag when you never pull the trigger?

I got a text in early May from Dirsch that he had got his tags in the mail that day. He wanted to know if I had received mine. I called him as I went out to the mailbox. I popped the door open on the box and grabbed the stack of mail and started to thumb through it. As I was thumbing through it, I saw the envelope I was looking for. It was on again for sure. We were both all geeked about our luck and the chance to get to hunt elk again.

During the time after the previous year's hunt and now, we had relocated from Michigan to Ohio. We live in a suburb of Columbus. The weather here is quite a bit more mild than Michigan. I told Dirsch that Payten and I had been riding quite a bit already. Payten has been my riding buddy for a long time! She started riding with me when she was seven or eight. If I was going for a ride, she would want to go, and I would ride with her from the house to the stop sign at the end of the road, then back to the house. That was a mile, and it also satisfied her. After that, I would go for my ride. As she got older, we would go a little farther. We would go to the stop sign, turn, and ride past the house to the other end of the road and back to the house. Then we were riding around the block which was a little over three miles. Now it has turned into if we don't ride twenty miles, then we haven't really even gone for a ride. I wonder how much longer before I can't keep up with her!

I told Dirsch to get after it. The clock was ticking. We talked about when we would go. What we settled on was I was going to fly out on September 6. Chuck would pick me up. I would spend the night at his place and get stuff around for the hunt. Dirsch would fly in on the seventh because the sixth is his wedding anniversary. We would hunt until the fifteenth and fly home on the sixteenth.

Chuck is awesome about letting us use his place as base camp and sharing what gear he has with me, stuff that I don't have the room to bring with me. The fact is, if I need it, and he has it, he lets me use it. Great to have people in your life you can count on! Chuck also feeds us well when we are there. I also love the smell of his place. Chuck heats with wood, pine wood to be exact. That smell brings back so many fond memories. The smell of his house is one of the things I look forward to every time I go out there. Anyhow, back to Chuck's stuff. I talked about Big Red and what a great truck she was. Chuck told me he got us a new truck to use this year. This ride was a white Ford Ranger that he had put the topper off of Big Red on. This ride was 4-wheel drive too, and Chuck said he had put a new fuel pump in and new tires all the way around. Chuck said she would be "race ready" for us when we got there. We decided before we got there we had to name the new ride, and Moby it was! Moby was a jump cab too, and it's always nice to have the extra room.

Dirsch and I kept in touch, tracking progress on new gear, like broadheads, bugles, decoys, and what the weather was going to be like as we were getting close to going. We were also tracking wildfires. It was an extremely dry year in Montana, and there were several wildfires burning across the state. One of them was close to one of the areas we liked to hunt. We decided that we should have a couple of backup places just in case. One of the spots we picked for a backup spot was one where Andrew had taken me before and had taken both

Dirsch and I one of the years we had gone out there. I can say every time I had been in there, we were into the elk. I stayed in close contact with Chuck, getting a lot of updates on the fires. There was a fire ban pretty much anywhere we would be hunting, and I told Dirsch it could get pretty cold at night with the ban in place.

We were both rounding into hunting shape, and I continued to rack up the miles on the bike. My goal was to get one thousand miles in before we left for the hunt. I was feeling great and felt I was in the best shape I had been in since I had started going back to Montana to hunt elk. Not long before we were to go, Chuck let me know they had some substantial rains come through and the fire we were concerned about was no longer burning and they were going to lift the fire ban in that area. That was some welcome news.

We were about a week from going, and it was "Move in Day" at Wright State. Payten would be attending school there for her freshman year. Wright State is just north of Dayton, Ohio. It's about an hour from home. We left early in the morning to get there at our scheduled time. If you have kids who have gone to college and lived on campus, you know the crazy, chaotic, yet organized day that move-in day is. Not knowing what to expect, it seemed at first to be a total chaos, but it was actually well planned out and organized given the sheer number of students getting moved in and how fast they made it happen. We got Payten moved in and unpacked to a level she could work with. We met her roommate, Halle, and her family. After all of that, we went out and got something to eat, then to the store to get the kid some grub and other things she would need. We got her back to her room, helped her get her stuff up there, hung around for about fifteen minutes, and then said our goodbyes and headed home.

It is a tough thing letting your kids grow up and go their own way. You always knew the day would come, but when it finally does, it is a good reality check, knowing you won't be right there to help them if they need you. That's when you have to hope they have paid close attention to what you have been trying to instill in them their whole life so they can make good decisions and fend for themselves. When we got home, it was hard for me, and I know it was just a little bit harder for Meg.

During the summer, I met a guy at the public shooting range at the metro park. His name is Mac. He is the best target shot I have ever met. The first time I ever saw him, I thought he was a whack job! He was walking up to the range with a sleeveless T-shirt on, ripped all the way down to his waist, pair of cowboy boots on with his pants bunched up in the tops of his boots and talking to himself. It took me a minute to realize he was on his phone talking on Bluetooth. We ended up striking up a conversation and yucked it up quite a bit. Mac's shooting was crazy good. He was hitting a single square piece of duct tape, maybe two inches by 3 inches, at fifty yards two to three times out of three shots, every time. I was shooting at the same piece of tape, and if I had three arrows within six inches of the tape, I was happy. I told him I could hardly even see the target, let alone the piece of tape. I let him know my sight just about covered the whole target. Mac looked at my sights and cracked up.

He asked, "How old is that sight?"

I said, "Maybe four or five years old."

He said, "Look at your sight pins and look at mine." His pins were tiny! One of my pins would make up two or three of his. "You need to spend some money and come out of the Dark Ages!"

Mac also recommended that I switch to some new smaller-diameter arrows with micro fletching, which means smaller feathers which are actually plastic vanes, to stabilize the arrow in flight. He said it would get me more speed and better penetration. I told him I was close to going on my trip and wasn't crazy about making a major change to my bow at a time like this.

Mac told me, "Just do it. You'll be happy. I'll help you get everything set up."

So against my better judgment, I bought a dozen arrows and a new sight two weeks before I left.

Mac met me at the range a couple of days later to help me get my bow sighted in. I needed his help to tweak the optical part of the sight that helps you make sure your form is on point. If you can't see the optic fully, you have a break in your form and can make the adjustment needed so your shot is true. After we got that set and with the new arrows, I had to adjust my sight bracket up a hair. The arrows were noticeably faster and were hitting a bit high at all of the distances out to fifty yards. It took a minute to get used to the new sight, but there was improvement for sure, even that very first time I shot it, especially at longer distances. I shot every day until I left and was very confident with the new setup. Mac also noticed some bad habits I had acquired over the years and cured me of my evil ways. He had made a big improvement in my shooting in a very short time, and I let him know how much I appreciated it.

I talked to Chuck, and he told me that the fires were dying down, thanks to some help from the Big Guy upstairs in the form of rain, and they were going to lift the fire ban in the entire western half of the state. I texted Dirsch that the ban was lifted and sent him a photo of my basement floor with all of my gear scattered all over it.

It was one week till fly day for me. Then the day before fly day, I texted him that the final packing was taking place and that I had somehow thrown my back out and I was in some serious pain. My excitement over the trip was being overshadowed by my back being out. Not a good place to be before a trip into the Rocky Mountains! I called a guy I work with, Tom, who does some back work, and he gave me a few things to try to relieve the pain. To my surprise, they made a big difference in a short time. I still bought a pack of back pain pills just in case but was feeling more optimistic about my situation.

September the sixth, fly day and my brother Scott's birthday! As I got out of bed, I can say my back was feeling pretty darn good. It was a bit sore but nothing like it had just a day or two before. I did a double-check of my checklist while I had my morning coffee. I got showered, dressed, loaded my gear, and headed to the airport. The airport is about half-an-hour drive from my place. I got there, parked, caught the bus to the terminal, checked in, got through security, and made my way to a place where a guy could purchase a legal beverage and purchased one! I texted Dirsch and asked him,

Are you drinking a beer waiting on a flight
to Montana?

He said,

No, but I did leave work early because I
have elk hunting on my mind.

He also told me he was jealous of me. I let him know my back
was doing much better, to which he said,

Good, 'cause you're gonna need it to pack
out all of the meat we're going to get.

We both felt like we had done all we could to be prepared, physically, mentally, and were both high on confidence.

I got on my flight and landed in Missoula around nine that
night. Chuck was there waiting for me. We grabbed my bags, loaded
them, and were on our way to his place. Once there, we went to his
basement and started to get what was stored down there that we
would need and hauled it upstairs. We visited and yucked it up for
way too long and went to bed way later than I had planned. The next
morning, we got up, and I made coffee, while Chuck made breakfast.
I texted Dirsch and let him know I was pretty much packed up and
would see him soon. His flight was to land at 1:20 p.m. Chuck and
I hung out and talked while I loaded Moby up, and at 12:45 p.m.,
I headed to the airport to get Dirsch. His flight was right on time.
We loaded his stuff up and headed to town to buy some stuff that we
needed from the local outdoor store before heading out.

CHAPTER 11

irsch was pretty set that he wanted to go to where we had
hunted with Andrew, and I had to say I agreed with his thought
process. I don't believe I had ever been in there without getting into
elk. We headed east until we hit our exit and got off. We got to the
frontage road and then onto the road that went up into the canyon,
then the mountain where we wanted to hunt. As we drove up the
canyon farther and farther, the road narrowed down and gets tight
before opening back up once you get a little higher up. We had driven
about three quarters of the way to where we wanted to go and had to
stop! The road was gone! It looked like the spring runoff had washed
it out to the point that even taking a motorcycle on what was left
would be spooky. There was no way we were going up that road in
Moby! What a kick in the pants! We had to regroup and adjust. We
decided to go to where we usually started our hunting trips, which
was a mere three-hour drive, and it was getting to be late afternoon.
This delay would put us getting to that camp spot well after dark. We
turned around and headed south to our new spot, but at this point,
it was all we had.

When we got there, thank God, no one was camped there. We
got the tent set up in the headlights and got a fire going, had some
grub, and went to bed shortly after that. Dirsch's phone woke us up
at five. We got out of the sleeping bags and to the back of the truck. It
is tradition to have coffee and oatmeal. So we did just that and made
our lunches, got our packs ready as well as our bows, and headed up
the long ridge as we had before. This is the location where the elk
don't bugle much, but the lack of bugling and sign, especially fresh

sign, wasn't building much confidence in either of us. We got back to camp without hearing or seeing a single elk or seeing any fresh droppings. That evening around the fire, we discussed what we were going to do. We decided to give it a go in the morning, but if things didn't pick up and convince us to stay, we were going to pack up and try to find a way into where we wanted to go in the first place.

Five o'clock, and the alarm went off. We were up and at 'em. We decided to hunt down today since hunting up yesterday wasn't good. We hiked out onto the ridge and watched the sun come up. It is hard to believe there are people who never watch the sunrise once in their lifetime. If you never have, I highly recommend it. It is good for the soul, a true blessing to witness. We worked our way down the ridge to the valley floor and back up the next ridge to the south. We took our time and called every now and then, to no avail.

Once again, we never saw or heard an elk or any fresh sign. That was it for us. We hoofed it back to camp, broke it down, and headed out to see if we could find a way into our original destination. It was a few hours' drive just to get back to where we could get started into where we wanted to be. We figured if everything went right, we could be setting up camp by dark. Then we thought, *What if everything doesn't go right?* That made us change our minds. We decided to drive to Chuck's place for the night, get a hot shower, a good meal, and a good night's sleep and look at Google Earth and maps to see if we couldn't set a route before going at it blind and wasting a bunch of time. We were down two days already; no need to make it three or four.

That night, we found what we thought was a solid way in on the back side of the mountain we planned on hunting. That was the plan, and we went to bed optimistic that we would make it in there the next day. We slept in a bit the next morning, and by the time we got all the stuff and ourselves ready, it was about noon when we left. It should only take us a couple of hours to get to where we wanted to be.

We got on the interstate and drove to the next exit past the usual one and got off. We took the frontage road to the canyon and headed up into the creek bottom and started to ascend up into the mountains. We had gone several miles when we reached the road we hoped would take us to where we wanted to be and turned up and continued on. It was in pretty good shape for a little while. The higher it went, the rougher it got and basically turned from a road into a two-track trail, with lots of ruts and bumps. I was driving, and Dirsch was the navigator. By tracking ourselves, it looked like we were getting close to the top of the ridge and the road we hoped would take us to our destination. The road on top was the same road that was washed out down below that wasn't passable. Based on what we were seeing or not seeing, which was tire tracks, we figured the area we were trying to get to may not have anyone in there due to how it had to be accessed, so we were optimistic about that.

We broke out into some open terrain and started up a steep hill. We were pretty much trailblazing at this point, but Moby was up for the challenge. We crested the top and started down the other side when Moby started to spit and sputter. It was bumpy, and we were bouncing as Moby finally stalled out on us altogether. Maybe she wasn't up for the challenge after all. We looked at each other with the "Oh crap" look on our faces. I am not mechanically inclined, but Dirsch has some knowledge. We popped the hood, and in short order, Dirsch figured out the carburetor wasn't getting any gas! We both were thinking the *fuel pump* Chuck had put in before we got there was bad. Lucky for us, we actually had service where we were dead in the water at. I called Chuck, and he couldn't believe the fuel pump wasn't working.

He said he had tried it out before he installed it, and it worked just fine. Chuck is extremely mechanically inclined. I told him all we knew was there was no gas getting to the carb, and we were dead in the water. He said he would get another pump and asked me where we were. We turned on the GPS and gave him our coordinates through text so he could put them in his GPS. We also told him how we had got to where we were at. He told us to unload the truck and take the topper off because we were going to have to lift the bed of the truck to get to the fuel tank because that's where the fuel pump was at. He said he would be there as soon as he could. We figured it would be at least an hour, most likely two, before he got to us.

We proceeded to unload the truck. We got all of the gear out of the truck and got the topper off. We were sitting on the tailgate of the truck. Dirsch had the owner's manual and was reading it to see if there was something that we could do to help ourselves.

During this time, I could hear a deer distress call and asked Dirsch if could hear it. He said he could and had seen a coyote up in the woods running around chasing something up there. I grabbed the pistol and headed that way. As I got closer, I could see the coyote was chasing a mule deer fawn, closely followed by the fawn's mother. I was about halfway there, and the coyote took the fawn down! The fawn's distress call went to another level at that time. It was much louder and more intense. I picked up my pace, and about that time, the doe got there and proceeded to thump that coyote with her front hooves, leaving some noticeable marks on the side of the coyote and some fur floating in the air. The coyote let go of the fawn and took off running with the doe in hot pursuit, swiping at the coyote as she chased it away from her fawn. As I got to where the fawn was, the doe noticed me and broke off her chase of the coyote and ran up on a small ridge and was standing there looking at me. The fawn was lying on the ground with its mouth wide open and foaming. It was panting hard. It didn't appear to have any wounds on it, just some slobber from the canine. When she stopped chasing the coyote, he turned his focus back to the fawn, turned, and was closing the distance fast. The coyote, as he was almost to the fawn, lowered his head, picked up his pace, with his tail straight out behind him totally unaware of my presence. When he had just about reached the fawn, I said as loud as I could, "What do you think you're doing?" That coyote turned inside out trying to get out of there. The coyote ran as fast as he could up and over the top of the hill out of sight. I backed off the fawn as it was catching its breath and to make sure the coyote didn't return. The doe made her way downhill to the fawn, and after a bit, the fawn stood up, and the two of them walked off together. Good deed for the day done, I headed back to the truck.

When I got there, Dirsch asked what happened, and I told him the story. He liked it and laughed about me spooking the coyote out of there. I started to think about our situation and how much time had passed since we had talked to Chuck and how much time we had left before it would be dark. It wasn't too much longer before we could hear the faint sound of an engine off in the distance. It had to be Chuck based on our location. Sure enough, as we looked toward the top of the hill, we could see the roof of Big Red cresting the hilltop.

Chuck rolled up on us and, with a disgusted fatherly look on his face, said, "What are you guys doing here?"

We laughed about that pretty hard and got right to work on Moby. Chuck got us working on unbolting the bed of the truck. Once that was done, the three of us lifted the bed and propped it up with a couple of logs Chuck rounded up. There was plenty of room to work, and it only took Chuck a couple of minutes to swap out the fuel pumps.

Chuck told Dirch, "Fire it up."

Dirsch turned the key, pumped the gas, and it cranked and cranked and cranked. Nothing! Chuck then thought it must be a bad module, so he grabbed one out of Big Red and plugged it into Moby, and Dirsch turned the key again—nothing. Dirsch was reading the troubleshooting chart again in regard to the carb not getting fuel. Chuck was sure it wasn't the module and for sure knew it wasn't the fuel pump because he tried it at the house before he left, and it worked fine. We were all frustrated at this point as the sun was approaching the horizon. Dirsch was reading out loud from the manual and, as he was reading, said something about the "emergency disconnect" for the fuel pump.

Chuck threw his head up with his eyes wide open and said, "Damn it!" He walked around the truck to the passenger side, opened the door, and got up under the dash. You could hear a click, and he said, "Fire it up, Dirsch!"

Dirsch turned the key, and Moby roared back to life. My buddy Dirsch is six foot three or four, and in the small cab of Moby, with all the bouncing around we were doing while trailblazing, his foot must have hit the disconnect, and it came unplugged.

What a relief! Chuck buttoned up the fuel pump, and we lowered the bed and bolted it back down. We got the topper on Moby.

Once we got back to that point, we basically just threw everything back in the truck to get moving again. We thanked Chuck. He headed back up over the hill out of sight. What a guy, what a friend. How many of you have that friend in your life? Someone who would drop what they are doing, drive to the middle of nowhere over something like that, laugh about it, and not think anything of it? The total downtime was about three and a half hours. Call Triple AAA, and see if they can help you out in a situation like that.

We kept heading in the direction of the road when we reached the next obstacle that awaited us. We were just below the road we needed. The road up to that road was steep, with lots of loose rock, and was washed out on both sides, with some ruts. It was uphill on the right side of the truck, and it was pretty much a cliff on the driver's side down to the creek bottom. Not really a cliff, but if we got off that side, it was going to be a long roll to the bottom. Dirsch got out to direct me the best he could. He walked to the top and was on the road up there. He yelled down to me that there were some serious ruts up there, bad enough that if I got the wheels in them, we would be stuck for sure!

He said, "You need to get up here and drive over the ruts till the wheels are far enough on the road that you can turn and straddle the ruts."

I nodded and backed Moby down the hill onto the flat at the bottom. I put Moby in 4-wheel drive low for the attempt and went. I ended up spinning out on the rocks when I was about halfway up. Now I had to back down on the loose rock without sliding off the downhill side. I inched my way, slipping and sliding back down the hill every time I hit the brakes, and backed far enough on the flat that I could get a good run at it. I stopped for a minute to gather myself and asked God to keep me safe, then hit the gas! My speed was much faster this time, and I was bouncing a bit and was doing a good job of staying out of the ruts on the hill. My momentum seemed to be enough to carry me to the top this time, barring any mishaps on the way. As I approached the top, Dirsch was giving me hand signals, like I was a fighter jet pilot landing on an aircraft carrier, of where I needed to go once I was over the ruts. I saw the ruts when I hit the road, and they were deep for sure. I turned left a little and crossed over the ruts at an angle, caught some good air off the seat during the process too, hit the high ground between the ruts, and came to a stop.

Dirsch said, "Good job!" and hopped back in.

I told him, "Nice job directing me!" At that point, we knew for sure we were hunting in the morning.

As we drove on the road, it started to drop down into the canyon where it was washed out, and I looked left and could see our road. I turned left onto the road. Even in the fading light, you could see clearly there were no truck tracks on the road.

Dirsch said, "I don't think anyone's been in here."

I said, "I believe you're right, sir."

We only had a couple of miles to go at that point. It was going to be another get to the camp spot after dark, put up the tent, go to sleep hungry deals. I drove up to the parking spot to make sure no one was there, and there wasn't. We turned around and drove back down the road to a wide spot out on the end of a ridge where the road came around the end of the ridge and pulled over. This was going to be base camp for the rest of the week. There was a nice flat spot on top of the ridge between the road where it came around the point to put the tent up. We got our pads and sleeping bags in the tent and got as much stuff ready as we could, then went to bed. We were worn out from the day's events!

CHAPTER 12

As I lay in my sleeping bag, I was filled with excitement at the thought that most likely, no one has been here hunting. It could be really good! I drifted off to sleep.

I woke up to the sound of the alarm on his phone going off. We had the house special for breakfast, packed our lunches, and filled our water bladders full. We buttoned things up around camp and headed down the road to the parking spot. It was about half a mile, and we parked the truck.

We got all of our stuff out, loaded our packs, grabbed our bows, turned on our headlamps, and took off. There was a peak that usually held elk, and that was the destination for the day, to get in there and hunt that area. We walked the road for about half a mile or more, then turned up to get on top of a small finger ridge that led to the main ridge that led to the mountain we wanted to hunt. As we hiked the finger ridge, we made it to the main ridge, and once we found an old logging road on top, I piled up a stack of rocks in that spot. I did it so if we got an elk and were coming out in the dark, we would see that pile of rocks and know we needed to turn right to take the finger ridge down to the road that went to the parking area. At that point on the main ridge, it didn't look like there is a finger ridge there going off to the right. It just looked like a wide spot on the main ridge.

I told Dirsch we could run into elk anywhere on the way in, but the mountain was usually where we had got into them when we had been in there before. I had set a pretty brisk pace on the way in because I was focused on the peak when Dirsch said he heard something moving off out in front of us. We stopped. I was thinking cattle because the ranchers put their cattle in the hills to graze in the summer and round them up in the fall. As we stood there, a herd of elk moved into the opening out ahead of us, out of bow range. There was a raghorn bull which is at least a two-and-a-half-year-old bull with branched antlers and a couple of spike horn bulls which are a year-and-a-half-old bulls and about a dozen cow and calf elk. The herd calmed down and moved off uphill to our left.

We talked, and Dirsch said, "We're moving too fast," and I agreed considering I was the one who said we could run into elk anywhere in here. We went into snail mode after that. No need to go blasting through the woods spooking anymore elk.

I told Dirsch, "If you think you hear anything, let me know 'cause I can't hear as well as you."

He said, "I will."

We waited about twenty minutes and headed in the general direction the elk had gone which was toward the peak we were headed to. Moving much slower now, we continued toward the peak. We didn't run onto the elk we had seen earlier but continued up the ridge, higher and higher.

We were working up one side of the ridge, and I told Dirsch, "I want to get up on top of this ridge to get an idea of how it is laid out in case we get into a bull up here during the week." Knowing the layout may help us in getting a bull if we got one going on the ridge.

He said, "Okay."

And we headed left to access the ridge top. We were in pines that were just over our heads and had gone about thirty yards when I spotted a mountain lion!

I said, "Cougar!"

Dirsch said, "Where?"

I said, "About forty yards," and was pointing with my left hand right at the cat. He had something pinned to the ground, and his back was to us. The cat was big and muscular! I believe it was a male based on his appearance. In that split second, Dirsch had pulled his pistol and was at the ready. I drew mine too just to be safe.

I couldn't see exactly what the cat had pinned down, but I knew for sure it wasn't a deer or elk or anything big because I couldn't see it at all. I figured a hare, grouse, or squirrel. The cat never looked our way. It just picked up his meal, growled, and walked off into the trees. When he growled, it made the hair stand up on the back of my neck. Have I mentioned I don't like cougars? This was the closest encounter I have ever had, and I'm sure it was for Dirsch too. And it was as close as I ever wanted to get to one for the rest of my life! Cougars can stalk right up on game and take down an animal as big as a bull elk by itself. The thoughts of having a souped-up hundred-and-fifty-pound wildcat on top of you is not a place I want to be. Dirsch and I were wide-eyed and on hyper alert. We talked about what a morning we had so far and continued on with our guns drawn for quite a ways. Once we holstered them, we continued to look behind us almost as much as in front of us for a while longer.

So far, this hunt was stacking up as one of the greatest of all time, and it was just the first morning. We stopped and were talking about the cat encounter again when we heard a bull bugle out in front of us down over the ridge to our right. It only sounded like it was a couple of hundred yards out. As we slowly worked our way toward the bull, we could hear that there were two bulls fighting down there. We decided to set up and see if we could get one of them interested in us. Dirsch moved toward the bulls, and I went behind him and was on top of the ridge to put Dirsch in between me and the bulls. That way, if we got one interested, it would be focused on me, not on where he was at, and I should be able to get the bull to walk within range of him.

I bugled and got a reply right back. That's a good thing! As I called, I could tell the bull was on the move, and I needed to reposition to get Dirsch in between us again. I moved about a hundred yards to my left. It was about 10:00 a.m. at this point. The bull would bugle every time I called, but his progress had stalled. He kept calling back from what sounded like the same position every time. After close to an hour and him responding every time I called, I thought, well, he was in a fighting mood earlier, so I grabbed a big stick, about four inches in diameter and six feet long, and started to beat the crap out of a sapling by me. This was in the hopes that the bull would hear that and think I was another bull ready to fight and

64

would make him mad enough to get him moving toward my location. I had tried everything else I could think of to that point. After I beat that tree for several minutes, I could see the bull below me moving from the left to the right. I was thinking he had to be real close to meeting my buddy Dirsch real soon. Not long after that, I heard Dirsch shoot, and it sounded like a solid hit. I stood there waiting to hear the crash of the bull going down or to see Dirsch motion me down to him, but nothing.

My curiosity got the best of me, and I started down that way slowly toward where Dirsch was. When I could see Dirsch, he was standing up looking downhill through his binoculars, then he would grab his rangefinder and look through it, then back to his binos.

When I got to him, I said, "Did you hit him good?"

He said, "My typical shot," which meant he hit him right behind the front shoulder, right where you want to hit one. Dirsch is a dead-eye no matter what weapon he is using. Mind you, typically, when you hit an elk, there it is, game over in short order. At this point, it had been several minutes since the shot. Dirsch pointed out the bull to me, and he was just standing there seventy yards down the hill.

I asked Dirsch if he might have been quartering toward him when he shot, and he only got one lung, or maybe he thought he had a better hit than he did because in the heat of the moment you can think you saw it one way, and you find out later you were completely wrong.

Dirsch said, "No, the bull was broadside as he walked by and only twelve yards away." He saw the arrow hit the bull right behind the shoulder. Dirsch did say he was at full draw for a really long time as the bull approached because it was open terrain and didn't want to spook the elk when he got in on him. He also said there was a giant bull with this one but hung up at a hundred yards, and this one had come right in without stopping. He said he thought about passing the bull he shot because of hopes the bigger one would come in. I told him I would have had a problem with that decision. He said he knew that, and that's why he shot.

On any elk bow hunt, it is reasonable to think that during the week, one of you will get a legit shot at killing an elk, and when that chance comes, you better take it because after that, your chances of getting a second shot drop drastically. Elk is great table fare and worth all the work and effort put in. To pass one up in the hopes of a bigger one almost always won't work out the way you wanted. I had seen the bull Dirsch shot, and he was a decent bull for sure and would be Dirsch's best bull.

Back to the bull! I said, "If you hit him where you said you did, and he's standing there like that, maybe he has the wound held shut, or slowed down, and that's why he's still standing up."

Dirsch said, "What do you think?"

I said, "Shoot him again."

The elk was in the open seventy yards away downhill and quartering away slightly. Dirsch agreed and readied for the shot. He drew his bow, settled in, and released the arrow. There aren't many times in your life you get to see something of perfection, but I can tell you that 70-yard shot was one! The arrow, when it left the bow, looked like it would sail over the bulls back by ten feet and disappear into the landscape. As it continued its flight, it slowly descended and hit the bull perfectly at the back of his ribcage right up into where you want a shot to go. The bull bolted on impact.

I said, "Nice shot, Dirsch. You smoked him!" Then we could see a huge cloud of dust rise up. "I believe your bull is down."

We high-fived and headed downhill to find the bull. When we got to where the bull had been, we saw good sign and took up the trail. As we descended, we were looking for blood and didn't see the bull lying dead in the middle of an old logging road.

You couldn't have picked a better place for a bull to go down. It was flat on a hillside with lots of room around him to be able to process him with ease. We took some time for photos and more high-fives. We told our sides of the story again, had a snack, and started on the work. I carry a tarp in my pack, and I got it out and laid it on the ground. We started to skin the elk on the side that was facing up. Once we got it skinned, I was taking it apart by the quarters and boning out the loins. I would pass the meat to Dirsch, and he would finish boning out the hind legs and shoulders. We then placed the meat in game bags to protect it. We would have to make two trips to get everything out. There was too much to carry in one trip, especially for a fifty-six-year-old man! Once we got our packs filled up, we hauled the rest of the meat we couldn't haul a few hundred yards down the road to hang it up in a tree away from the kill sight. Dirsch got on my shoulders and we tied a rock to our rope and he threw it up over a branch about fifteen feet up in the tree. We pulled the meat up till it reached the branch and tied it off to a tree close to that tree. You never want to return to a kill sight if you don't have too. When you leave, others may lay claim to your kill, and they don't take kindly to you coming back to take what they have claimed as their own away from them—they being *grizzlies*!

We were walking back up the road to get our packs and a bull sounded off right below where we had just quartered Dirsch's bull, and we weren't being quiet at all during the process. As we reached where our packs were, Dirsch could see it was the bigger bull that had been with the one he shot. We looked at each other, and Dirsch said," Let's go kill him!"

I grabbed my bow, and Dirsch grabbed the bugle. I started down over the hillside toward the bull and Dirsch uphill away from the bull to get me in between the two of them. As I inched my way down, I could see there were elk everywhere in this draw. The draw had a small stream running down it, and along the stream was thick and shady, with lots to graze on. It made perfect sense why they were holed up in there. I went as far as I could with so many elk and so many eyes that are always on the lookout for danger, and I set up. I looked back at Dirsch and gave him a hand sign to go ahead and call. I was ready.

The big bull was chasing his cows up and down the drainage. I would be able to see him for a few minutes, then he would run down the stream chasing one of the cows out of sight for a little while, then he would come rushing back up and chase another one around for a bit then disappear into the creek bottom.

Dirsch threw out the first bugle, and the bull fired right back before he had finished the bugle. A really good sign to be sure. After a while, Dirsch bugled again, and the bull fired right back again. I wanted Dirsch to pick up his calling, but I had repositioned and no longer had visual contact with him. At that point, I got out my cow call and called a couple of times in an effort to make the bull think that he was losing one of his cows to the intruder, hoping he would come my way to herd her back up and push her into the bottom with the rest of his herd. The bull bulged and headed my way. The bull was at sixty yards, which is a distance I had been comfortable with in the past. At fifty-six years old, my sight wasn't as good as it had been, and I didn't have a sixty-yard pin on my bow anymore. I had imposed a fifty-yard limit on myself and was going to stick to it for a couple of reasons. My thoughts were it was day one and we knew he was in there and we had five more days to get on him and get him into a closer range. He didn't know we were in there, so he didn't know he was being hunted. And the last reason was I had failed to keep myself hydrated with everything that was going on and now was at the point my hands were cramping up and was pretty sure I wouldn't be able to draw my bow and make an accurate shot, so I passed on the shot. The bull was magnificent! He was a fully mature six-by-six bull, which means he had six points on each side of his rack. His antlers were massive. They were wide, and his main beams were long with average tines. He was a brute of a bull.

I waited for the bull to move off chasing one of his girlfriends and eased myself out of there. We still had a lot of work to do and a long way to go. I got to where Dirsch was. He asked if I had shot. I said no and told him why. After I got to thinking about it, the last time I could remember actually drinking any water was after we had bumped into the cougar hours before. The day had been so action packed and full of excitement I just got caught up in it all and hadn't thought about it, and that is a great example of just how quick you can get yourself into trouble in the mountains. I was in no danger because I had water to drink and just needed to sit down and drink it, which I did, but it goes to show how you can be doing fine one minute, then realize you have a problem. With the environment that is Montana, with high country arid conditions, I knew better than to neglect my hydration, yet here I was, dehydrated.

We decided to haul the meat we had packed up back to camp, then hunt our way back in the next morning and see if we couldn't get on the bull again or another bull. If we didn't get into any action, we would get the rest of the meat, break camp, and head for Chuck's place to care for the meat. The plan would be to get everything taken care of with Dirsch's elk, regroup, get a good night's sleep, and get up and head out around 3 a.m. that would put us back at the parking area right on time to head back in to hunt the next morning.

After drinking most of my water and having a bite to eat, I was feeling much better, and we loaded up and started the climb back up the mountainside to the top of the ridge. There is nothing quite like pawing your way up the side of the Rocky Mountains with a hundred-pound backpack full of meat strapped to your back. Quite the workout! This is where the hours of riding and weight training pays off. My pack was so heavy my shoulder straps were digging into my shoulders, and I could feel my heart pounding in my head, sweat running down my face. As Chuck would say, I was a "dribbling mess." I had a boned-out hind quarter in my pack with a loin draped over the top of it with each end stuffed into my side pouches and a front shoulder boned out tied to the outside of my pack. Dirsch had the other loin and the inner loins in his pack, along with all the gear out of my pack and his gear, with the head and cape, which is a load by itself to carry, along with his bow. Coming out heavy for sure. Dirsch couldn't use his hands to get up the mountainside because he had to hang on to the bull's antlers to keep the head and cape on top of his pack. The elk head had Dirsch's head sticking out in front of him with his neck extended. It didn't look very comfortable at all. Good time for sure!

We crested the top. We took a break and planned the rest of the hike out. We talked about where we would stop for breaks along the way, but once we got back up and moving, we only stopped one more time on the three-mile hike out because it was just easier to keep going. We followed the ridge back to the rock pile on the road and dropped down the ridge to the road the truck was on and made it back to the truck. What a relief it was to finally get out from under those loads for good! We drove the short distance back to camp. It was dusk by then, quite the day in the field. We were both tired but jazzed up at the same time. We glugged down a couple of celebratory beers and talked about the events of the day. We felt other than the elk we bumped when we first got on the ridge, the elk had no idea we had been in there after them. The big cat we saw didn't jump on us. Dirsch got his best bull ever, we got some good exercise, and we still had five days to go. It had been as close to a perfect day as you can get.

Dinner that night was elk on the open fire, with potatoes and onions in the fire with a couple more cold ones. It was a great day, a great hunt. We ate like kings and slept like babies!

CHAPTER 13

U p the next morning, we had breakfast and only packed a snack and water for the day because we knew we were on a mission. We would hunt our way in, then get the rest of the meat, then hike out and head to Chuck's. We knew our packs were going to be much lighter today which was good. My shoulders were a bit tender after the previous day. We could get service on the ridge every now and then, and we called Chuck and let him know we got one and would be coming out of the hills to his place to get things taken care of. We let him know we would be there sometime in the afternoon.

We hunted our way into where we had been the day before. We heard a couple of bugles, had some casual encounters but nothing to really get us excited. It was late morning when we decided to go get the rest of the meat and start back. We hiked to the spot on top of the ridge above the elk carcass, and both of us glassed the kill sight with our binos, looking for any sign that there might be something down there that had claimed the kill. Once we felt pretty good the area was clear, we descended down at an angle toward the rest of the meat hanging a few hundred yards from the carcass.

As we worked lower and lower moving to the right, we kept glassing back toward the kill sight making sure there wasn't a predator that may have found the kill in the night. We still didn't see anything and moved quickly to where the meat was hanging and cut it down, loaded it up, and we were headed back up the ridge in no time. We were laughing at how light our packs were today compared to yesterday's load. I will say it did still feel like work though. We were both happy but had some tired legs. We made it back to camp by noon, never stopping once.

When we got back to camp, we were breaking stuff down and loading up. Dirsch was looking for a better way out than the way we came in. Neither of us wanted to try to traverse those ruts while turning downhill with the condition of that road and the thought of possibly going off the downhill side of the road. As I was finishing up with loading, Dirsch said he thought he had found a better way out that was all road the whole way. I looked at his phone, and it looked solid. When we had come in and were on the road that turned into us trailblazing, there was a road we had passed on the way up that turned off to the left. It looked like Dirsch had found a connection to that road, and that connection was right at the end of the ridge we were camped on fifty yards away. If this worked out, it would be slick, with nowhere near the risk as the way we had come in and a much faster way in for in the morning.

Dirsch is great at using his phone as a tool to navigate but not so good at getting around by using his *inner compass* in the wild. I tell you this because the day before, as we were hiking in sometime before he got his bull and after we had the run-in with the cougar, he said to me, "Every day, ask me which way camp is throughout the day."

I asked, "Why?"

He said, "I don't know how you get around out here, and I want to know how you do it. I just follow you around and don't really pay attention to where we are."

Well, after he said that, I said "Okay, which way is camp?" with a smile on my face.

Dirsch said with a smile on his face, "Right here, right now?"

I said, "Yep, which way?"

He stood there thinking, then threw his arm out pointing and said, "Camp's that way!"

I said, "Final answer?"

He said, "Yep, final answer."

I pointed in the exact opposite direction and said, "Camp's that way."

He said, "Really?"

I said, "Really!" We laughed for a minute. "I navigate around by using landmarks when I'm in Montana."

I used this example: If we left camp, and there was a peak to my left, when I was returning to camp, that peak should be on my right. And I picked out other landmarks in the area to mark where I was. I let him know there was a tree on the ridge that the top was broken off of it and there was a piece of bark sticking up off the top and it has a perfect hole through it the size of a baseball; that's a landmark. And then there's a salt lick the rancher put out for his cattle farther down the ridge. That's a landmark. And the next landmark was, on our way back out, I had the pile of rocks on the logging road that would tell me to turn right to go down to the road the truck was parked on, if that makes sense. He said it did.

I told him, "You need to pay more attention to your surroundings if you want to navigate the way I do."

That day when we were in there, Dirsch wasn't much closer to getting it right, but I was glad he was trying to learn because you never know when you may need that skill.

We were all set to try out our new route. Everything was packed up, and we headed to the end of the ridge for the first turn. There was a bunch of ribbons—blue, black, and white checkered—tied to the branches of a sapling where that road took off from the main road. This road, you could see, was much less traveled than the one we were camped on. We took the right and drove on.

Dirsch was following the road on his phone and said, "It looks like it's good the whole way."

The road was heading in the right direction. It would be a wait and see if it actually crossed over to the other side of the canyon where the road was that goes to the creek bottom. If that happened, then we were good for sure. The road was bumpy and full of rocks but still much better than the way we had come in. The road did indeed swing around to the north and crossed over to the road we needed to descend into the creek bottom, proving to be the road we had driven by on the way up into the hills a couple of days before.

Dirsch's new route was faster and much safer. It took us an hour and a half to get to Chuck's place from our campsite.

Once we got to Chuck's place, we took care of the meat first, then unloaded everything to take stock of our provisions, then repacked everything in preparation for the next morning. I was repacking stuff, and Dirsch was skinning out his bull's head. He decided that he wasn't going to get it mounted. Chuck volunteered to do a European mount for Dirsch, which is where the skinned-out skull is bleached snow white and mounted like that on the wall or on a plaque on the wall. Chuck did a great job at it, and I knew it would look great in Dirsch's lodge. We were making great progress in our preparations for our three o'clock departure in the morning.

Chuck got some antelope out of his freezer, and that would be dinner. I've heard people say antelope is terrible. I can say I've never had a bad experience with it. Chuck said the key to having good antelope is to get it skinned and cooled down as fast as you can after the kill. I've never killed one, but Chuck has killed several, and based on the meals I've had with him, I would say he knows what he's talking about. He seasoned the meat and cooked it over an open wood fire that night. It was fantastic! Dirsch and I got showers that night, and I took one in the morning to help wake me up and get the blood pumping. We pulled out of Chuck's place at 3:30 a.m. based on what we knew about our new way in and how long it had taken us to get to Chuck's place. We should be at the parking spot at five, and that would be perfect for us to start our hunt in.

I had an Upland Game Bird license in my pocket that I was itching to use. We hadn't seen any grouse on either of the first two days, but I was optimistic we would get into some soon.

I love shooting grouse with my bow. It is good practice because they are small targets, and they are delicious. I'm always looking to have a feathered friend over for dinner.

The hike up the ridge was pretty quiet. We called a few times but got no responses. We hadn't made it to where we had got into the elk before, but we decided to sit down and take a break. It was still early with lots of day and hunting ahead of us. The spot we sat down was a perfect spot to listen for a bull sounding off. We should be able to hear them even if they were a long way off, pinpoint them, and make a plan to move on them. We had been sitting there for a short time, and Dirsch said he could hear something below us. After he said that, I told him I could hear it too. We could hear sticks breaking and what seemed to be a lot of ruckus going on down below us. We were sitting where a finger ridge came off of the main ridge and went down into a little saddle and then out to a point that dropped down into a bigger valley. It sounded like there were elk in the saddle, and they were very active, running around. The wind was blowing from our right to out left, so we devised a plan to hike to our left, with the wind at our back to keep it in our favor, then drop down the hillside and approach the elk from downwind and see if we could get things stirred up more than it sounded like they were already.

We dropped over the hillside to the level we figured the elk were at and slowly began to move into the wind until we felt we were close enough to set up and start calling. We started to pick up movement in the timber ahead of us and looked for a spot to set up. The area was pretty open, and there were several big pines. We picked out one with a downfall at the base and got set up there. We could see elk at our level, above, and below us too. They were all moving all over the place. It was hard to know which direction to focus on.

Dirsch asked, "Do you think the cows are being herded by bulls?"

I wasn't really sure what was going on. It seemed like there was an awful lot of movement for it to just be a bull herding.

I told him, "I'm not sure what's going on."

We threw out a couple of cow calls, and the elk began to scatter, and we were trying to figure out why. There was no way they had winded us, nor anyway they had picked up any movement because we were sitting still, only moving to call, but something was definitely up! There was a good-size opening below us on a bench, and elk were moving through the opening. We saw several spike horn bulls and some decent raghorn bulls along with several cows and calves and one really nice mature bull, and it wasn't the one from the first day. We were happy to know there were several bulls in the area and more than one big bull in the area. Still unsure what was going

75

on, we continued to call. The elk below us were looking up our way, and we were hoping a bull would head our way.

Dirsch suddenly said, "Wolf, coyote, cougar."

I said, "Which one?"

He said, "Cougar!"

I said, "Where?"

He said, "Right in front of us!"

I asked him to be more specific on where. We were on a rise above the bench, and I couldn't see a cougar anywhere.

He asked me, "Do you see that small tree right in front of us?"

I said, "Yep"

He said, "Look to the left of it along the crest of the hill."

Bingo! I saw it! All you could see was the big cat's head sticking up over the crest of the hill looking right at us. He was no more than twenty yards away! I told Dirsch to get his phone out and take some pictures as I drew the .45 and got a bead on the cat. He blended in perfectly with the color of the fall grass. The cat must have been chasing the elk around and heard us calling and worked his way right in on us. The adrenaline was flowing and fixing to go to the next level as the cat came up over the edge, swung to our left, and now was moving in on us. The cat got to about twenty feet from us and stopped. He was locked eye to eye with me. He knew I was something alive but not sure what.

Dirsch said "What do you want to do?" in a normal tone of voice which I thought would make the cat bolt, but he just stayed locked on me.

I said, "Throw a stick at him."

Dirsch picked up a good-size stick and threw it in the cat's direction. It went right in front of the cat's face. It never even flinched, still locked eye to eye with me.

Dirsch said, "Now what?"

I said, "Hit him with a stick."

Dirsch picked up another good-size chunk and let it go. It hit the cat right in the head! Upon impact, the cat bolted to our right and, in three bounds, was about fifty yards away, then gone without ever making a sound!

Dirsch and I looked at each other with wide eyes and the expression of "Holy crap!" on our faces.

Dirsch said, "Do you think you could have shot him?"

I said, "I would have shot."

He said, "No, do you think you could have shot him?"

I said, "I don't know, but I would have shot!"

The fact of the matter was, after seeing the cat exit stage right in the fashion he did, I know now he could have jumped on us as soon as he crested the hill at our level. What an amazing beast and what a show of amazing physical abilities that really blew our minds. When you watch a cat like that chasing down its prey on TV, you just can't get a real appreciation of just how impressive they are or just how much ground they are covering each bound! That still amazes me to this day, one of the greatest things I have ever seen with my eyes.

After all of this, there were still elk below us, and there was a raghorn bull barking down there due to the presence of the cougar. They do that as a warning call to other elk that there is danger present, and this guy was on it nonstop. A lot of the elk had worked their way left on the bench below us, and we figured the rest would follow suit, so we decided to move uphill out of their sight, then turn to the left and head that way to get the wind in our favor again and drop down to the bench in hopes they would come in with some soft calling to herd back up. We got over what we figured was far enough and dropped down and got on the bench and got set up.

Dirsch got set up, and I worked toward where the elk were. I was about fifty or sixty yards from Dirsch. I signaled back at him, and he called softly a couple of times. The bull was still barking over in the opening and had been the entire time. Dirsch called again, and after that round of calls, I could hear something rapidly approaching me from behind. The sound wasn't very loud, but in my mind, the sound pulled up the vision of a cat with big padded feet, equipped with very sharp claws approaching me from behind to take me down! I spun around only to see nothing! I could still hear the sound and was looking hard in the direction it was coming from when I picked up movement in the treetops. It was an osprey dive bombing its way down over the hillside in my direction.

I thought, *What the heck is he doing, and why is he up here?*

I had never seen an osprey in the mountains like this. The only place I ever remember seeing them was around lakes. I thought they were fishers. Anyhow, the bird had his wings fixed, his legs were hanging low, and the sound I was hearing was the wind going over his wings as he went over and under branches and around trees as he was coming downhill. I looked forward in his line of travel and I could see a grouse sitting up on a branch in a tree near me and it was looking down at me. I don't know if that grouse could see the expression on my face change when I realized what was about to happen to him or her, but the osprey arrived right about that time and took the grouse right off of the branch. The grouse was more than the osprey could fly with, and the osprey immediately started to lose altitude.

I was thinking to myself, *Oh, this is going to be a classic crash and burn!*

The osprey was going down fast and flew that grouse head-first right into a log. Lights out! That grouse never moved an inch after impact. The osprey stood there on the ground with his chest all puffed up looking proud of himself.

I said to Dirsch "Go get a picture of that!" as I headed that way. I could have cared less about elk at that moment. As we approached the scene of the crime, the osprey flew up into the tree above the carnage, looking down at us, keeping a close eye on us. I don't consider myself a bossy person. The reason I told Dirsch to go get a photo was he had a better phone than me. Now he may not echo that thought about me being a bossy person, but he was the camera guy, and I was the protection during the shoot.

The grouse was big and would make a great meal for both of us. As we talked about it, the osprey was sitting above looking down as if he could tell what we were talking about and seemed to have a look of concern in his eyes. After the discussion, we decided the osprey earned the kill, and it was his. We moved off in the direction the elk had gone in hopes of catching up to them or another herd in our travels. On our way back to camp, we decided to swing back through the area where the grouse met his demise. When we got there, all we found was feathers everywhere. The carcass was gone; the osprey was gone. We both hoped the osprey got his meal, but we'll never know for sure. We hunted all the way back and made it a full day.

When we got back to camp, we made dinner and had a couple of cold ones and hit the sack. Tomorrow was another day. The days had been warm and sunny, and the nights were clear and getting colder by the day. The next day, there was a chance of rain, so we double-checked our rain gear, and I always had the tarp to huddle under if it got too bad.

CHAPTER 14

The morning broke colder than it had been. We ate, packed our lunches, and headed up the mountain. The plan for the day was to venture deeper into the area than we had up to this point, look at some new land and see if we could get me a bull. We were trying to hunt smart so we weren't educating the elk that they were being hunted. We had bumped a handful, but there was a ton of elk in there, so every day was a great opportunity to get into a good bull.

As we made our way up the ridge, we could hear some bugling going on, so we worked our way toward where it was coming from. We were on the east side of the ridge overlooking an area we hadn't been in, and it was becoming clear we had found some more elk to hunt. The bull we were hearing was just down off of the ridge top, and we were catching a glimpse of him every now and then as he was running back and forth on a logging road. It looked like there were a few cows with him. Knowing that, we figured that we most likely wouldn't be able to get him to leave them to come to us, so every time he moved off pushing his cows around, I would inch lower and lower toward the logging road. Every time the bull moved off, and we bugled, he would come back to the same spot and bugle back at us. My plan was to get to a spot that would have him in range and an opening big enough to get a shot at him.

The bull sounded off, and it sounded like he was coming back. I was in a pretty good spot and could see the bull approaching through the trees on the logging road. I was ready! Did I mention that there was a chance of rain for the day? As the bull approached with the front moving in, the wind swirled, and that was the end of that encounter.

While all of this was going on, there was another bull that had called back to us a few times from below us to our left out on a finger ridge that came off of the main ridge. So we at least knew who the next contestant was on, Elk Love Connection! We didn't have him pinpointed, but we had a general idea of where he was, so we headed that way.

We didn't know if he was on the ridge or in the draw closest to us. With the wind blowing through the trees and never knowing what direction the bull could be facing, it can be difficult to locate them precisely. We knew he was close, but that exact distance was hard to figure out. We descended down onto the ridge and gave a few cow calls. Nothing! We waited and called again. Nothing! He was gone. We had to have bumped him. We weren't having much luck today in our new area, to say the least. We moved back up to the top of the ridge. We had been stopped for about a minute, and I was glassing downhill.

I said to Dirsch, "I can see a herd of elk way down there moving through an opening fast."

They were probably four hundred yards away. I got Dirsch on to where they were moving through, and I don't know how many moved through the opening, but it was at least fifty for sure. I don't think that we were the cause of their flight, but on this day, who could know for sure? September the thirteenth was the kind of day that if you were watching yourself from a ways off, you would think to yourself, *Those guys don't know a thing about elk hunting!* That day was the first day after being in there for four days that I knew we bumped elk, and it was adding up to be quite a few. Despite bumping elk after elk today, I still felt that we would get it done because of the amount of encounters we had since being in the area. We just needed the right elk in the right situation. We had the rest of today and two more full days, lots of hunting to do yet.

We moved farther on the ridge and had gone about another half of a mile, and the rain showed up in force. We happened to be in a spot where there were smaller lodgepole pines and found a couple that were broken off a few feet up from the ground which was perfect for a ready-made frame to put the tarp over and hunker down for a bit and wait it out. We got everything set up in short order and crawled under the tarp. We talked about what a great hunt it had been so far.

I told Dirsch, "This is the single greatest hunt I have ever been on in my life as far as success, encounters, excitement, action, and I can't wait to see what the rest of the week has to offer."

We stayed under the tarp until the rain let up and then we began to hunt our way back to camp. On the way back, we ran into some grouse, and I was lucky enough to take one with my bow. Dinner was set for the evening. The biggest thing to do now was figure out what side dishes to have!

When we arrived back at camp, the clouds were clearing, and it was going to be a cold one for sure. I was busy boning out the bird as Dirsch was cutting potatoes and onions. We wrapped the meat in foil with olive oil and some seasonings, the potatoes and onions the same. We got a fire going and were busy gathering extra wood because it was cooling off fast. When the fire had burned down to a good bed of coals, we put the grub on the coals. It didn't take long with the pile of coals we had before the food was done. Dirsch had decided on a pack of chicken and noodles as a side dish to go with the spuds and onions and Raspberry Cobbler for dessert. It was going to be a feast in the Rockies again! We ate dinner and kept the fire going hot and stuck it out as long as we could, but we were tired. It was cold and getting colder, so we decided to turn in for the night.

When you're in the mountains, one thing that is a must is a headlamp for many reasons. It makes things like going to bed easier. I got in the tent before Dirsch this night. Having that headlamp made getting my sleeping pad and sleeping bag ready as well as getting undressed and having the next day's clothes in a handy spot to get dressed much easier, as well as getting out of the tent after getting dressed in the morning. My headlamp is the last thing I take off every day. Once off, it went in the corner of the tent by my head with other things I may need, like my gun, keys to the truck, knife, boots—you know, things you may need in a hurry. Dirsch and I had it down and could get in and out of the tent in short order ready to go.

As I was lying in my sleeping bag with my eyes shut, Dirsch came in the tent, with his headlamp on of course. I was getting flashes of light from him looking around but didn't dwell on it because I was tired and was going to kill my elk tomorrow, or the next day. I drifted off to sleep in no time.

CHAPTER 15

When the alarm went off, one thing was abundantly clear. It was the coldest it had been by far since the trip started. We rolled out, got dressed, fired Moby up to warm up. We had breakfast and coffee in Moby that morning and made our lunches after. We drove to the parking spot loaded up and headed out. I was happy to be walking to generate some heat and warm up. It was September 14, my mom's birthday! As we climbed, it was crisp and clear. All of the clouds had settled down in the valleys overnight as if they were too heavy for the cold thin air to hold up in the sky. It looked like the mountains had cotton stuffed in every draw, nook, and cranny.

We decided on our way uphill that we would swing by and check on the big bull that was with the bull Dirsch had killed. We had left him alone for a few days. We worked our way toward the draw he hung out in and seemed to call home. We usually got to where we wanted to be and would wait around and let the hunt present itself to us. Elk typically feed downhill in the evenings and water, then feed back uphill to bed and chew their cud during the day. As we approached the draw, he bugled. He was ahead and slightly above us. The wind was not good and was blowing in his direction. Worried he would get our scent, we scrambled to the left and around the side of the ridge to get out of the wind. We talked about the wind and how it wasn't good, so we decided to hit the deck and wait for it to get more consistent so we could use it to our advantage. We hadn't called, and as long as we had got around the ridge in time, chances were good the bull had no idea we were around.

There was something different about the bull today. The bull was bugling more and more and running back and forth on the ridge, and it sounded like he was raking the trees up there pretty good. He was worked up and getting more and more worked up all on his own.

I told Dirsch, "When the wind is better, we're going up there and killing him!"

Dirsch went and sat down on a log a short way from me. I looked around and found my own log and walked over to it and sat down on it in a side-saddle type position. The log was on the ground on the left end of it and was propped up off of the ground on the right side about four feet up off the ground at its highest point. I had my backpack on, and my bow was across my lap. I was enjoying the morning sun and the moment while I looked around and listened to the bull bugle. As I was looking up and down the ridge, keeping an eye out for any elk that the bull may pull past us, I turned my head to the right and felt a big "pop" in the back left side of my head! I had a sensation of a wave going from the left to the right side of the back of my head.

I thought, *What was that?* Then my bow slipped from my hands and fell to the ground as I started to lose consciousness. My backpack was pulling me over backward as I grabbed on to the log. My feet were on the ground, and my butt was on the log as the upper part of my body was almost parallel to the ground off the backside of the log. I hung on and came out of it for a second and sat back up. I was looking down at the ground and couldn't make it out. That's when a second wave hit me, and I started to black out again. It was at this point I remember thinking to myself, *Man, you're in a world of shit right now!* I was scared to death of what was coming next and got a big rush of adrenaline and sat up again. My hands were shaking uncontrollably, not because of being scared. I had no control over them. I still couldn't see, and now I was thinking, *Is this it? I'm dying right here, right now.*

It was at that moment the only thing I wanted was to be able to see Meg and the girls so I could tell them how much I love them one last time. The reality that I was never going to see them again was devastating for me! I told God, *I'm sorry for my sins, and please*

85

take care of my wife and girls. As I was coming to grips of the reality of my mortality coming to an end and accepting it, my vision came back crystal clear! I looked over at Dirsch, worried about him getting out of there okay. He had been doing better with his navigation but still hadn't been able to point right in the direction of the truck or camp. Dirsch had no idea what was going on. I figured that I must have had an aneurysm burst. I couldn't think of anything else it could have been.

I gathered myself and stood up. I looked like a sapling in a stiff breeze. I was swaying all over the place. I thought, *How am I going to get to him and let him know what's going on?* It never occurred to me to say, "Hey I have a problem." I staggered over to him; my balance was way off. I tapped him on the shoulder. Dirsch looked up at me, and I said, "Something popped in my head. I'm having a hard time staying conscious. I'm really scared. We need to go. You gotta get me to the hospital."

I will never forget him looking up at me, and he said, "Are you shitting me? The bull is right up there."

I said, "No."

I think it was then that he could tell I wasn't joking and said, "Okay, let's go. Give me your pack and bow."

I said, "Look, if you think I'm going the wrong way, tell me and tell me why so we can talk about it because I don't think I have any time to be wasting."

Dirsch said, "Okay."

I figured we were between three and four miles from the truck, another ten miles in the mountains, and forty miles from Missoula.

I fully expected to fall flat on my face dead in front of Dirsch on the way out. As we had walked a short distance, I asked Dirsch, "If I die, will you please make sure to tell Meg and the girls just how much I love them?"

He said, "Yes, but you can tell them yourself because you're going to be fine."

At that time, I am sure I wasn't as optimistic about my future as he was. We had walked about a mile, and Dirsch said, "I think you're going the wrong way."

I said, "Why's that?"

He said, "I don't ever remember going down this ridge."

I said, "We never went down it, but we came up it the first day we were in here."

I told him how it was laid out and what we would see, and after a short way into it, he agreed we were good.

On the walk out, I was talking to God. I asked him, *Please spare me, at least until I can see my family again and tell them I love them. I will do whatever you want me to do if I can just see them again!* I can tell you, as I was walking and talking to God, I did not feel alone. I knew Dirsch was with me, and I was grateful that he was. Every step of the way, it felt as if someone had their hand on my back, and in my head, I heard, *One foot in front of the other*, over and over again.

With each step, I felt better because I knew we were getting closer to the truck, and we reached a point where I knew for sure Dirsch knew where he was and he would be okay if I went down for the count. And at least my body would be going back home. I had been walking with my hands on the sides of my head because it literally felt as though it was going to explode. It hurt so bad.

Dirsch asked me, "Do you want to sit down for a bit?"

I told him, "No." I felt that if I sat down, I wouldn't get back up. "If we had a cordless drill, I would let you drill a hole in my head to release the pressure." It hurt that bad. I've had migraine headaches and knew how debilitating they can be, but they were little league compared to this one.

I could barely keep my eyes open anymore because of the headache, and the sun was blinding me. I was stumbling from time to time and tripping over the rocks. I could feel that my mind wasn't in a good place.

We were about two to two and a half miles into the hike, and Dirsch said, "Hey, you're going the wrong way!" He didn't say he thought I was; he said I was!

I asked him, "Why's that?"

Dirsch said, "You just stepped right over that pile of rocks you stacked up in the middle of the road so we would know to turn right here."

I looked at the rocks and asked him "You sure that's them?" knowing myself it was but still asking the question.

Dirsch said, "Yeah, that's them."

We turned and headed down to the road that led to the truck. Once we hit the road, I knew for sure my body would be going home if I passed.

I thought, If I go down now, Dirsch can drag my body to the gate, leave me there and hike up to the truck, get it, and drive to the gate and load me up. We made the gate and kept going till we made the truck. For some reason that morning, we loaded everything into the bed of the truck, so the truck was loaded and ready to go. Once we got to the truck, Dirsch and I talked about the route out on the roads. I told him it would be four right-hand turns, the first being at the end of the point where we had camped. Then he would stay right until we hit the T in the road that went downhill left to right. Then to the creek bottom, take a right out to the frontage road, then to the interstate.

CHAPTER 16

A s we started to roll, Dirsch said, "Do you hear that?"
The left rear wheel was squeaking.

I said, "Yes, it probably has dust in it from sitting around for days."

In the mountains, the higher up you are, the worse the roads get, and we were up in the mountains quite a ways. As we were going, progress was slow at first.

The lower we got, the better the roads got and the faster we could go. The faster we went, the more noise the wheel was making. By the time we got to the creek bottom, it was pretty loud, and we were going about thirty-five miles per hour on that road. We hit the frontage road, and speed picked up to forty-five to fifty miles an hour, and the wheel was making a ton of noise.

I had service and called Chuck and told him what had happened, and we were going to St. Pats Hospital in Missoula. I asked him to call the hospital and tell them we were coming in and what happened. I had given Chuck all of the details, in hopes they may have an idea what was wrong with me and could prepare for us getting there. He said he would, and he would see us there.

We hit the on-ramp for the interstate, and the speed limit is eighty! Dirsch kicked her down, and we got on the highway. Moby didn't sound good, and Dirsch was having problems just going sixty. Dirsch asked if we should stop and check it out. I told him if he wanted to stop, to go ahead, but I couldn't help him. I couldn't even open my eyes anymore. The light was blinding, and it just increased the pain level higher when I opened them. We had this conversation on the frontage road too.

At this point, Dirsch said, "Screw it. We're going for it!"

As we drove down the road, Moby would just take off, going all over the place Dirsch had his hands full for sure. Now he's got a friend and a truck neither functioning well. I can only imagine what the other drivers were thinking about what was going on in our truck based on how it was making its way down the road.

I told Dirsch, "If I die or become unconscious, you want the second exit in Missoula. There will be a hospital sign for St. Pats. Get off there, turn left. It's like a few blocks on the right. Chuck will be there."

We got to the exit, somehow got off, turned left, and we could see the hospital and the signs for emergency. We rolled up on Chuck who was standing there waving his arms for us.

Chuck opened the door when we stopped and said, "Gus, what's up with the truck?"

I told him I wasn't sure, something with the left rear tire.

He told me, "I could hear you guys coming off the interstate. Stay here. They're coming out to get you."

They were there pretty quick and wheeled me inside and right into a room. They took some vitals and were hooking me up to some other things, then off for a CT scan. When I got back to the room, Chuck came into the room. Now Chuck is a very animated guy. When he came in, his eyes couldn't have been any wider open without tearing the skin in the corners of his eyes. His mouth was hanging open, and he said to me, "Shit, Gus, three of the lugs and the nuts were missing off of the wheel, and I unscrewed the last two with my hand. They were barely hanging on to the threads. I can't believe you guys made it here."

Chuck and Dirsch went back outside. I knew I was still in trouble, but at least I was in the right place. It had been about four hours since my brain blew up. The doctor came into the room and was asking me questions about what had happened—about the headache, if I had nausea, if I had seen any bright flashes of light. I answered no to all except for the last one. The flashes of light!

I had asked Dirsch on the way up the mountain that morning on one of our stops, "What were you looking for in the tent last night?"

He said, "Nothing. I wasn't looking around. I came in the tent, got in my sleeping bag, turned off my headlamp, and went to sleep."

I didn't think a thing of it until the doctor asked that question. The doctor said that was a warning sign for an aneurysm. I asked the nurse if she would get Chuck and Dirsch for me, which she did.

When they got to the room, the doctor said, "You were the one with him?"

Dirsch said, "I was."

The doctor said, "How did you get him here?"

Dirsch said, "We drove."

The doctor said, "No, how did you get him to the truck? I understand you were quite a ways for the truck when this happened."

Dirsch said, "He walked."

The doctor said, "I don't see how that can be with the injury he has."

Dirsch said, "Well, he walked the whole way."

The doctor said, "The CT scan did indeed show a bleed on the brain, and we have called for Life Flight to transport him to Spokane, Washington. I just don't see how he could have walked out of there with the injury he sustained. He should have fallen over dead the instant it ruptured." He went on to say, "I don't believe in miracles, but in his case, I have no other explanation as to why he is still alive and still functioning."

Dirsch looked surprised when the doctor said I had a bleed on the brain. He said he had googled bad headache in the mountains, and it said altitude sickness. And he thought that is what I had. It appears the aneurysm that ruptured was on the artery that feeds the brain.

I asked Chuck to call Megan and let her know what was going on. He said he would and went out to call her. When they called Life Flight, it was in Billings, Montana, and would be there in twenty-five minutes. Impressive, to say the least. Billings is a long, long drive from Missoula going eighty miles an hour or faster.

Meg said when Chuck called, she was out with her girlfriends. She said when Chuck told her what was going on, and I was in the hospital with a really bad headache, Meg said her response was, "Okay, so?" Chuck said he thought she should call the hospital.

Right after they hung up, Meg's phone rang again. It was the doctor. The doctor explained what had happened and told Meg she needed to come out to Spokane. There was nothing Meg could do to get a flight that day. The best she could do was the next morning.

Life Flight had arrived, and in the time before that, both Dirsch and Chuck were in the room with me and thought that I would be more comfortable if they took my boots off. I have to say it sounded like a pretty good idea to me. I will say that after eight days of your feet stewing in your boots, the smell can be a bit overwhelming! When they pulled my boots off, it felt wonderful! I will add it also smelled like sweaty roadkill in there. It was rancid! I remember two workers strolling by my room. The door was open, and they had that "nose crinkled up, sour puss" face; you know, the one that says "Oh god, what is that?" look! We had a good laugh over that.

The Life Flight crew came into the room and took over! They were getting information from the doctors and telling them in return what they wanted them to do to get me ready for transport. I already had an IV in my right arm. They asked for another in my left arm. They also asked for a couple of syringes of something to be brought in. Once they got them in the room, the medic shot the first one in my left arm. That one hit right away! I felt like I melted into my bed. After that, he sent the second one, and it was, "Ladies and gentlemen, Elvis has left the building!" I have always wanted to go for a helicopter ride, just not in this fashion. I can vaguely remember them putting me into the helicopter, and I remember in-flight talking to the medic briefly, but other than that, the next thing I remember was them taking me out of the helicopter in Spokane.

Before we left, the crew offered for one of the guys to go along with me. Both were very interested, but they had to get Moby and Chuck's ride back up the Blackfoot to Chuck's place with all of the gear in her. I found out they were able to get the two lugs back on the wheel and limped ole' Moby all the way there, which from the hospital would have been about fifteen to eighteen miles. Once they got there and got everything taken care of, they got cleaned up and drove over to Spokane.

CHAPTER 17

I had been flown to Sacred Heart Hospital in Spokane. Sacred Heart is where people in the Pacific Northwest get flown to when they suffer an aneurysm. They are known for their outstanding staff and great surgeons they have there for taking care of people in my situation.

Given the remarkable set of circumstances that had occurred that could have stopped my progress but didn't, another one was about to happen! Providence Sacred Heart Hospital in Spokane has a neurosurgeon, Dr. Carlson. When I reached the hospital, he was off on vacation. The staff looked me over and evaluated my situation. They then called Dr. Carlson and told him about me. He hadn't left yet for his vacation and wasn't to leave for another couple of days. After they informed him about me and my situation, he said he would come in the morning and do my surgery. Another doctor put a drain in my head for the night to relieve some of the pressure from the fluid and blood building up in my skull. I had suffered a subarachnoid hemorrhage. The aneurysm that ruptured was on the artery that goes to my brain and was the reason the doctor in Missoula had said that I should have fallen over dead when it happened.

When you have a rupture in your brain like the one I had, it comes with the "thunderclap" headache. I have had several migraine headaches in my life and know just how debilitating they can be, with the loss of vision, nausea, and the pain of the headache, but I'm here to tell you the headache from a ruptured aneurysm makes a migraine seem like little league. What makes it so much worse is the blood from the rupture has to go somewhere, and where it is going is in between your brain and the membrane that protects your brain and is pulling the membrane off of your brain. The pressure in your head is unreal; it literally feels like it will explode.

Chuck and Dirsch arrived. Talking to Dirsch after, he said when he came into my room with the nurse, he got a little emotional when he saw me lying there and how I looked. He said there was stuff coming out of me everywhere. I was on a respirator, there was a drain in my head, multiple IVs, heart monitor, and some other things too.

Dirsch said, "The nurse reached over and took my hand and said, 'Your friend is going to be fine.'" Dirsch said he said back to her, "He doesn't look like it to me."

She then said, "He's right where he needs to be."

When he told me that, I thought, *What a beautiful thing for her to do for someone in a moment like that!* Dirsch said it was hard to believe that I had gone from walking and talking to lying in a bed looking like I was on life support in the short amount of time that had passed since they took me on Life Flight.

The next morning arrived, which I wasn't aware of, and it was surgery day. By this time, word of my situation had spread and had reached family and friends. On the day of my surgery, Dr. Carlson would be doing a craniotomy, where a piece of my skull would be removed to allow my brain to swell, as well as placing a PICA clip on my artery to secure the blowout. The clip was a tiny titanium clip that closely resembles an alligator clip. Once in place it was a permanent fixture.

My dad, Larry; my sisters, Karen and Linda; Dirsch and Chuck were there for the surgery. After the surgery, Dr. Carlson came out of the OR to talk to them.

My sister Karen asked him, "How's he doing?"

Dr. Carlson said, "Your brother is going to be fine."

Karen said, "You mean he's going to live and be fine or have issues or what?"

Dr. Carlson said, "Your brother is going to be fine. The injury was massive, and he shouldn't have survived it. There was a huge blood clot in the area of the rupture that I believe slowed down the bleeding, but even with that, it still should have been fatal." Dr.

Carlson did go on his vacation after the surgery, and I began the process of healing and rehabilitating.

Following my surgery, the same day, I developed my first problem—hydrocephalus, or water on the brain. This increases intracranial pressure, which has its own name, cerebral edema. It was also noted by Dr. Carlson that the subarachnoid hemorrhage was progressing into my ventricular system, which is the four interconnecting cavities of the brain. I was placed on vasospasm watch, and the drain was in place to relieve the pressure in my head.

With aneurysms, 40 percent of people who have them rupture fall over dead at that moment. Another 15 percent die on the way to the hospital. Then after they reach help, there is the issue of vasospasms that can happen. This is the narrowing of the blood vessels, which reduces blood flow, that can bring on a stroke. Sixty-six percent of people who survive to this point suffer from effects from vasospasms.

Meg arrived in Spokane around 1:00 p.m. the day of my surgery and made her way to the hospital. I'm not sure how long she was there and can only imagine how tired she must have been based on her last twenty-four hours. At some point, she made it to her hotel room for the night.

The next day, the number one thing noted on the "problem list" was vasospasms watch. I was confused but otherwise noted as being "neurologically intact"! They sent me for a CT scan that showed no vasospasms noted, but the CT scan did reveal there was a second aneurysm in my brain, noted as "unsecured" and about two millimeters in size. With the hemorrhage progressing into my ventricular system, they were treating that with nimodipine, a medicine that is used to reduce the brain damage from blood from the hemorrhage. I was moved to a "high risk" status at this point and noted as being "critically ill." I was to be closely monitored going forward. They were also treating me with anticoagulants for blood clots, and I was noted from the results of my bloodwork as having developed "leukocytosis," which means my white blood cell count was elevated. The leukocytosis most likely was brought on from having had my surgery.

During the time since my surgery, one of the things that they were doing was waking me up every hour to ask me questions to see where I was mentally. The questions were really basic questions that should be easy to answer, but in my state, they were anything but easy! They would ask me my name, date of birth, how old I was, if I knew where I was, if I knew why I was there, if I knew what happened—basic stuff, right? I had the biggest problem with where I was for sure.

The next day, I was noted as still being confused but as doing "fantastic." I had an angiogram to get a good look at the blood vessels in my brain. They go in your groin and use your vascular system to access your brain. Then they put a dye in so your vessels can be seen by x-ray. They can tell if you have had a stroke from the procedure and if there are any bleeds on the brain and check the repair site where the clip was placed. They did find that I showed signs of strokes in the corpus callosum area of my brain. The corpus callosum is a C-shaped nerve bundle. It is the largest collection of white matter tissue found in the brain. White matter is nerve fibers, called axons, that connect nerve cells, and they are covered by myelin, a type of fat that gives white matter its white color. The report showed that even though there had been mini strokes in that area, they likely were of no consequence. I was able to follow commands and showed no focal deficits, which are signs of stroke. My body movements were good, no vertigo or eye movement disorder. I was still confused as to where I was and the date. The last place I could remember being was Montana. The plan was to continue with vasospasm watch and treat to prevent seizure.

The date today is September 18, four days in the hospital now. My sister Karen came to visit me today.

I had my CT scan this morning, and it showed there were infarcts in my brain. Infarcts are areas of the brain that have died due to lack of blood flow. The doctor noted in my notes, a "high probability" of acute clinically significant deterioration. This was the first time that note showed up in my records. Physical therapy came in today and had me up out of bed taking steps forward and backward at my bedside. My balance was noted as being good in the sitting position and fair while standing. I wore a fall prevention strap around my body so they could help correct balance issues while I was standing.

I also had my first visit today with my speech therapist. I was given an initial assessment and scored "Below" the mean, which indicated I was mildly impaired. My vision was good, memory and attention were "moderately impaired." All in all, not bad for a guy whose brain blew up. After all of that excitement, I was worn-out, and once I got back in bed, I was out.

I mentioned Karen had come to see me today. She is a believer in Zen! As Meg described it to me, Karen was standing over me at the side of my bed as I slept and was performing Zen over me! Since I wasn't awake for this, I will do the best I can to describe Meg's version of how it went. Karen would hold her hands above her head and bring them downward and spread them outward along my body; one moving toward my head, the other toward my feet. Then she would bring them back together and up and over her head. In the process of doing this, each movement was accompanied with its own sound. Wish, wosh, wish, wosh, wish, wosh! On and on.

Meg told me about this, and I laughed and said, "If I would have woken up during that, I would have looked at her and said, 'What in the world are you doing?'" Since I didn't wake up during that time, I can say in my situation at that time I'd take the Zen session and was glad she loves me enough to have done that for me—sibling love!

The following morning, the vasospasm watch continued, and now I had another problem—acute encephalopathy, which is an acute global, functional alteration of my mental status due to systemic factors. It is reversible when caught and treated. They continued with anti-seizure meds. I still had the drain in my head for the water on the brain, which the medical staff was leaning toward placement of a shunt for a permanent fix to the problem because it didn't appear to be getting any better on its own. The physical therapist showed up, and I was noted as being "reluctantly agreeable" to doing therapy. I had terrible pain today from my surgery in my head and neck. I did set a new world record, for me at least. I walked twenty feet, with a fall guard on. Good thing because I had some serious issues with my balance when turning around.

My gait was noted as "slow and cautious" by the physical therapist, and my posture was slumped forward. I did some seated exercises and was really spent. The therapist wanted me to sit upright in a chair for thirty minutes or more a day. To say I wasn't onboard with that program was an understatement. After therapy, I just wanted to get back in bed and go to sleep. My head hurt bad all of the time, but when my body was in an upright position, it was a whole other level of pain. Thirty minutes? Are you kidding me? I didn't like being in a chair for a minute, let alone thirty of them. My room was pitch-black almost all of the time. I couldn't take light of any kind. Light made my headache much more intense. Once therapy was over, it was lights out, curtains drawn, back to darkness.

According to Meg and Karen, one thing I was very consistent about was every few minutes in my darkened chamber, I would open my eyes and ask, "Where am I?"

They would say, "You're in the hospital."

To which, I would say, "What happened?"

Then they would say, "You had an aneurysm in your head burst."

Then I guess I would raise my eyebrows and say, "Oh."

Then on to the next three minutes. They said they would start laughing as soon as I opened my eyes because they knew what was coming.

CHAPTER 18

September 20, Maroon Five Day, we had tickets to go, but someone had to go and mess up those plans! Plan for the day was the neurosurgeon was going to do a shunt placement this morning. With a pending CT scan, it was noted the need for the shunt was due to a collection of fluid on the left side of my brain due to brain sag caused by the fluid and blood leaking through a tear in the dura mater. My brain could no longer float in its fluid. The brain can't feel pain, but the resulting sag pulls on the tendons and muscles across the head that worsens when the person is in a position of being upright causing extreme pain and is slightly relieved when a person lies down. This is why I liked my bed and hated my chair! The dura mater is the third and outermost layer around the brain and holds the fluid the brain floats in.

The shunt was placed, and later on, PT came and tested me for communication and cognition. They said I had good attention for a five-minute span and was able to hit 80 percent accuracy for problem-solving tasks. Not bad after having the shunt placed, and all of the results were in line with where I had been up to the placement.

The next day, they did another angiogram, which showed that I had a "significant vasospasm," so I was on vasospasm watch with euvolemia, meaning fluid balance, which means the water in my brain needs to be controlled. It was at this point where they began to increase my blood pressure due to the vasospasm. They moved my systolic pressure up over 150. Systolic pressure is the force of your blood against the artery walls as your heart beats. This rise in pressure is to help push back against the vasospasms as they try to contract my vessels. At this point, I was not showing any improvement in my condition after the placement of the shunt.

I was disoriented as to where I was still. I thought I was in Ohio and couldn't recall where I had been hunting before being in the hospital. I got the year right, and it was noted by the therapist, I was using humor to cover for my lack of awareness! I got cleared to start PT and OT again, and there was now talk about sending me to a rehab facility, which Meg was in agreement with.

My wife, I can't imagine what it must have been like for her to sit there every day wondering what she would be left with at the end of this. Every time the team would do something to help my condition, I seemed to be going in the other direction. My dad, Karen, and Chuck all said what a tough woman Meg was. Karen said that Meg was on top of things and made sure that everyone who came to see me was following the sterile guidelines. Karen said she only saw Meg cry for about half a minute one time. Then she gathered herself, straightened her outfit, and moved on. That's my wife! She is a rock, has a great head on her shoulders, and she's a fighter! How lucky I am to have her as my wife and partner in life!

During all of this, I set a new all-time record during PT. I walked seventy-five feet at a nice slow pace due to my balance issues. I sat in the chair and remembered that Meg and I were interviewed about our house layout for when I got home for possible home PT and the overall safety of the house for me.

I was sent for another angiogram later that day to put medicine in my arteries. They treated all four of my vessels and had noted that if my condition worsened, that I may need angioplasty under general anesthesia. Angioplasty is where they go in your groin up into the brain to open up your vessels to get the blood flowing better through the use of a ballooning type device.

September 22, still on vasospasm watch with euvolemia balance going on. My hyperdrive had now been raised to over 160 minimum blood pressure due to the angiogram showing that I had suffered a significant spasm in the back circulation system in my brain. I was awake and still confused at times. There was more conversation today about having the angioplasty, if I continued on my current path.

A team came into my room to sterilize it. The decision had been made to insert a PICC line, which stands for peripherally inserted central catheter. It is a line that is put in a vein in the arm that runs from there to a large vein near the heart. Once the room was sterilized, the team came in and did the placement of the line. The line is placed when meds need to be delivered directly into the system, and the treatment plan requires frequent injections and blood draws, which mine did.

The next day, I was noted as being "stable" for the last twenty-four hours. I was awake and less confused than the previous days. Today, I got another tube placed in me, a feeding tube! I hadn't eaten anything in nine days and was losing weight to the point I was determined to be "anorexic." That's a term that I never thought would be used in reference to me, but here I was rocking my new title.

Another adjustment was made today. My hyperdrive was moved to over 170. I had another vasospasm that was found during my angiogram. This one was located in the vertebrobasilar system, which supplies blood to the brain, and is a critical arterial supply to the spinal cord brainstem as well as the cerebellum, thalamus, and occipital lobes. This event was the deciding factor in them performing the angioplasty. The process was set up for the next day. I didn't have PT today as my blood pressure was raging at over 170 that had me in a bigger funk than before.

On September 24, the angioplasty was successfully performed. I was still in ICU, and after my afternoon doctor's visit, it was noted that I showed "no significant changes" at that point.

The next morning, I did have a change. I now was running a fever, noted at 101.5. The team called for a febrile panculture. This is done to help in determining the cause of the fever. I also was given a new hyperdrive number. It was moved to over 180. As usual, the vasospasm watch continued, and I was back on PT and ST. The physical therapist noted me as being "apathetic" toward my session and that I was depressed, and I was! I'm not a person who gets sick, and this was getting to me. I'm used to being on the go and doing things.

I walked seventy-five feet in therapy again and was not doing so well with the finger-to-nose task as well as the heel to shin. My balance was not good. I was noted as being slow in performing every-thing, even just getting to the edge of my bed to get out of it. I was noted as having "not much change" since the last session. One change today during the session was my blood pressure went over the 200 mark for the first time! I sat in the chair for my required time, then got back into bed. The bed was in the upright position, and as I was sitting there, I asked for a drink. After they brought me my drink, I started drinking it and could feel something in the back of my throat! I thought, *What is that?* and grabbed my feeding tube and pulled it out!

I looked at Meg and asked, "What the hell is that thing?"

She said, "That's a feeding tube."

I said, "Why do I have a feeding tube?"

Meg said, "Because you won't eat."

The nurse came in and wasn't happy. She asked why I had pulled it out. I told her I took a drink and could feel it and didn't know what it was and pulled it out. So they put it back in!

When they put it back in, Karen and Bonnie were both over to see me, and Bonnie said to Karen, "I'll bet you $100 he pulls that one out too."

The one they put in this time caused great discomfort if you try to pull it out.

Karen said, "Ya think so?"

Bonnie said, "Oh yeah, you watch."

September 26, I started the day off with a chest x-ray. The x-ray showed I now have atelectasis, which is a partial or complete collapse of an entire lung or a lobe of a lung. This is due to having alveoli, which are small air sacs that deflate or fill with fluid. This is common after surgery. They now want me to sit in the chair three times a day, *Booo*, and possibly a trip outside. Vasospasm watch continued.

PT gave me an assessment test today too. The last test was on the eighteenth when I tested as being mild to moderately declined in memory, language, and attention. My results today showed I was more impaired than before. I scored a ten out of thirty. Normal range is twenty-six out of thirty. I now show a decreased working memory and don't even know my own name, was reading numbers backward, had diminished attention, and did not do as well on visual tasks. I continued to have balance issues that required me to have increased assistance when doing things. I was also now having extreme difficulty during dual tasks in high-stimulation environments. On a positive note, I was cooperative with my therapist and did voice my frustration with my ongoing ICU stay. The staff were now talking about ramping up all of my therapies unless I started to make some significant gains.

CHAPTER 19

September 27, the first thing noted today was I was more awake and alert! They were planning on taking me outside today. Meg thought it would be good for me to go out and get some fresh air and may help me to be in a totally different environment that I had been in for the last two weeks, maybe spark something in me! Meg would be coming along on the trip.

From time to time now, my room wasn't in black-hole mode. They moved my bed in my room around and opened the curtains so I could see outside, in hopes that it may stimulate me and help pull me out of my funk! I love being outside as much as possible, and I can tell you I was less than excited about my planned trip outside today.

On the trip outside, it was sunny with a definite chill in the air. I was in a wheelchair because of my diminished endurance and the total amount of gear I was hooked up to all of the time. I had a blanket over my shoulders to help keep me warm. There was a male nurse moving all of my gear, and a female nurse was pushing me in the chair. Meg was talking to me and trying to get me to notice things and was also taking a few photos of me. I will say in those pictures, I was definitely showing the signs of not eating in a while, and I was also showing signs of not enjoying my trip. I had the sour puss on big time! She must have forgotten to say smile before snapping them off. It was way too bright for me after hibernating in my dark cave for so long. My head hurt more than normal, and even with the blanket, I was a bit cold. I can say now that trip was one of the things I do remember about my stay in the hospital and maybe, even though not recognized at the time, the start of some positive change coming.

When we got back to my room, one of the nurses brought in a spirometer. This is a device that is used to exercise your lungs. It helps to prevent pneumonia. They wanted me to use it once an hour for several breaths. The nurse noted that I was "extremely suspicious" of the device. I was refusing to use it or to even try it. You just put your mouth on the tube and draw a deep breath. There is a ball in the tube, and as you draw a breath, the ball lifts up in the tube. The tube is clear plastic and is marked with lines to keep track of progress in how high it is lifting off. The nurse kept trying to get me to do it, but I wouldn't.

Meg said, "Here, let me show you how to do it."

She took the spirometer from me and put it up to her mouth and began to inhale. The ball lifted and settled back down. I lost my mind!

I said, "Meg, I can't believe you of all people would do that!"

The nurse, surprised at my outburst, said to Meg, "What's the problem with him and the spirometer?"

Meg was cracking up uncontrollably, and the nurse was even more confused now. Meg, while gasping for air, said, "He thinks it's a bong!"

Now they both were cracking up, but I wasn't. I did think it was a bong and was worried we would get pulled for a random drug screen at work and get fired! This moment has been the cause of many laughs since that time and is also one of the things I remember from my stay.

Another thing was Chuck came to see me today. He and I played cribbage during his visit. I have no idea if I played it right or not, but I think I must have been close because he would have let me know if I wasn't and would have accused me of cheating. I'm pretty sure I won the game too! The visit lifted my spirits, and I was happy to see him.

The team had noted me as being able to follow the conversation today in my notes, and I was laughing at humor. I told them my pain level was a nine out of ten, but they noted I seemed more comfortable than that. They continued with my hyperdrive on my blood pressure, keeping it above 180 now. They wanted increased neuro checks during the night. I was still considered a high risk for neurological deterioration in the event of more vasospasms. I knew my name today and what year it was but not where I was or why, still confused and still not eating. They were also planning on removing my stitches from my head the next day, thirty-five in all.

The next day, during my morning doctor's visit, I was noted as being more engaged, still confused with memory deficits. Hyperdrive was to continue. Occupational therapy came in and had me do my A trials. It took me forty-one seconds which sounds good, but normal is thirty-two seconds. I couldn't complete my B trials after trying for three minutes. I was able to do the sample problem but couldn't get past the confusion of a full page of problems. It was like I was trying to solve all of them at once. They were recommending discharge, with at home therapy. They set some goals for me. One was to be able to dress myself. That's a good one, right? Second was to be able to complete ten minutes of tasks with no voice commands to stay on task. Third was to be able to stand for twenty minutes.

The rehab facility called and said they had a bed for me as soon as I was medically stable. During the morning visit, it was noted I still had a decreased appetite and confusion. I thought it was October but was able to correct it with cues. I knew I lived in Columbus but needed help to remember I was in Spokane.

One of the things we would do to help me with my issues in therapy was the therapist would give me a letter and would ask me to give her as many things as I could that started with that letter. Then they would ask me to name as many names as I could that started with the same letter. Today's letter was *F*!

I had sixty seconds total, thirty to do each task, which would really push me to use my brain. The therapist asked if I was ready. I said yes. At this point, I was trying to stockpile as many words as I can that start with *F* in my head.

She said, "Go!"

"Fruit, food, fire, firetruck, fox, fan..."

Thirty seconds had gone by, and she said, "Names!"

"Frank, Frankie, Fred, Fredrica, Fergie, Fergalicious, Fran—"

"Time's up!"

I was sitting there thinking, *I killed that!*

Meg and the therapist were sitting there laughing at me. I was trying to figure out what's so funny, and they couldn't catch their breath long enough to tell me. I guess I'll never know what it was! The therapist noted I understood memory strategies but demonstrated decreased awareness for their need. She also noted I showed lack of awareness and insight into my deficits. I got a third of my daily living problems on my own and needed cues to get the other two thirds. I'm sure after the full day I had, that must have had some effect on my performance. I sat in the chair for the required time, and my bed was calling out to me. I got into bed and got a drink.

Up until this time, I only had brief moments of clarity that I can recall. Most of my time was spent wondering if purple is a fruit like orange is. As I was sitting in my bed, with the back of the bed raised looking at the wall where the door to my room was, I saw my daughter Preslie walk into the doorway and stop. Then Payten walked into the doorway and was standing beside Preslie. I know I didn't know much, but I can tell you I knew those were my girls! At first, I was really wondering if I was really seeing them or if I was just having a dream or hallucination or something like that. Then I saw them whispering back and forth to each other and laughing at me. That's when I knew for sure it was them, and they were really standing there. I felt as though I was in a perpetual dream where I couldn't figure out what was really going on, but this was real! They walked in the room and over to me. They both hugged me, and we exchanged "I love yous." My spirit was soaring! Meg said her sister Michelle had made their trip happen in hopes that it would maybe help snap me out of my haze. I have thanked Michelle for what she did for us, but I can never express to her how much I appreciate her for doing this. It meant and still means the world to me!

I had my stitches removed today, so that was good. I couldn't see the incision site, but I knew my head was still killing me. The nurse came into my room. Time to sit in the chair again. I got out of bed and into the chair.

It wasn't long after the nurse left, and I said to Preslie, "Hey, Pres, help me get back in bed."

She said, "Nope, can't do that!"

I said, "Come on, Pres!"

Her reply was "No can do!"

I couldn't believe it! She wasn't going to budge on it either! She said she would help me back into bed when my time was up. The nerve! My brief moment of clarity faded off into another fog.

The next day arrived, and my room was alive with activity. I was asked my questions by the nurse. During my journey, I had been all over the place when asked if I knew where I was. I had been in DuBois, Pennsylvania, my hometown; Brookville, Pennsylvania, no idea why; Columbus, Ohio, where I live now; Montana; Spokane, Washington; and even Urethra, California!

When I threw that one out, the nurse came back with "I'll bet it's warm there!"

I said I didn't know about that. She asked me what I was doing there. I said, "Hunting!"

She asked, "For what?"

To which, I replied, "The Holy Grail!" Meg and the nurse had another great laugh on me.

I couldn't get my age right. I was anywhere from my twenties to my early sixties. I was usually close on the year, off by a year, one way or the other. Meg would always try to remind me to look at the grease board in my room. A lot of the answers were on it, but I couldn't even remember to do that. I was also like a powder keg with a short fast-burning fuse! I could go off at any time over anything. I lost it on Meg and the girls one time when they switched the channel on the TV, and I most likely wasn't watching it anyhow.

When I first started my journey, I used to get my vasospasm medicine in the form of a pill. I don't know how many times I took it in pill form, but in one of my moments of clarity, I remember seeing the size of that pill and thinking, *There is no chance I can swallow that thing!* It was at least an inch long, maybe a bit longer. It was as big as the Wooly Bear Caterpillar! I told the nurse I would try to take it but wasn't sure I could get it down. Meg and my sister Karen were there during this. I put the pill in my mouth and got a big gulp of water and sent it. Things started out okay, but about halfway down, it turned sideways and stopped! I started to gag and knew then there was little to no chance of it going down.

I said, "I'm going to puke. Give me the trash can."

The nurse was trying to get me one of those little barf bags but not fast enough for me. I could tell the pill was about to return to sender in a big way, with a lot more force than it went down with, and that little bag wasn't going to hold what was coming.

I yelled, "Trash can now!"

Meg or Karen handed me the trash can right then, and the pill left me at about 200 psi.

After that, I was given my vasospasm medicine in liquid form. That tasted terrible! I told Meg that stuff tasted like ground-up horse hooves and cod liver oil. Now I've never tasted horse hooves, but I have cod liver oil, and that was my best guess as to what it tasted like!

I know I yelled at some staff members, and one even refused to work with me afterward. I felt bad about that and give my sincere apology to those I upset or offended. That's not who or how I was in a normal state. I can say the staff at Sacred Heart would do anything and everything in their power to get anyone back to being healthy, and I am forever grateful to all of them for what they did for me and the excellent care I was given.

Here's one more blurry story from today. That night, Penn State was playing Ohio State in football. We watched the game in the black hole, which was my room. In my mind, I had it that this was just some type of exhibition game with some new scoring system in place for it. I do remember that Penn State was winning but wound up losing at the end of the game. I didn't care though because it was only an exhibition game.

CHAPTER 20

September 29. It had now been five days since my last vasospasm. That's a good thing! Vasospasm watch continued. I was drinking on my own but still not eating. It had been sixteen days since I ate last. I rated my headache as a four out of ten today. Pretty uneventful day for the most part. The girls did say that when they were out, that every day I would say "Are we all going to get cleaned up and go out for dinner?" several times over and over. They played along I think, knowing that I would forget sooner or later about going. I was still over the moon about having the girls there though.

The next day, I was diagnosed with cerebral salt wasting. This occurs in about 30 percent of people who have a subarachnoid hemorrhage. This is another thing that can lead to death, and proper diagnosis is critical of the etiology. An incorrect diagnosis can cause significant morbidity and mortality. Etiology means the cause. My salt levels were out of whack, which could become fatal if misdiagnosed and the treatment is not correct for the situation. It can also cause disease of the central nervous system. So I was to have frequent neuro checks after the diagnosis. They still wanted me to do my "bong" several times a day when I was awake. My hyperdrive was down to 160 or higher for vasospasm prevention. My daily CT scan showed that my rupture was now secure, and they would now start me on a prophylaxis to prevent any blood clots, or DVT. I was now taking salt tablets for my CSW and had my PT and OT increased.

One last thing from today, remember the new feeding tube they installed? When Bonnie said to Karen, "I'll bet you $100 he pulls that one out too"? Well, me never being one to disappoint, I pulled it out! I can tell you for sure it was very unpleasant!

The nurse asked me like the time before, "Why did you do that?"

I told her, "I could feel something in the back of my throat," and I asked, "Why do you keep putting it in there?"

She said, "Because you won't eat."

I said, "Bring me some food. I'll eat it."

She asked, "What do you want?"

I said, "Some fruit."

She brought me some fruit, and I ate it. That was the end of the feeding tube.

On October 1, after my morning check, it was noted by the doctor that my condition continued to improve. I still had some confusion, but it was much better than it had been. It was also noted that my eating was "markedly improved." Funny how a little pain and a pep talk can motivate someone.

During my OT, they noted me as "much brighter effect." I was making jokes and laughing with the therapist. I told her I was feeling mentally and physically better. I could get from my bed to the chair and from the chair to the bed without help but was still wearing the fall-assist belt. I was able to complete a higher level worksheet on my med's management and was able to work for fifteen minutes on a task without a break.

After therapy and lunch, I went for a walk with a nurse. His name is Graham. I really enjoyed my time when he was around.

As we were walking, I was joking with him, and he said, "Oh, you got jokes today and really seem to be doing good. Let's ask your questions."

I said, "Okay."

Graham asked me my questions, and he said, "Hey, you got them all right."

I said, "That's good, right?"

He said, "That's great."

I said, "Including this time, how many times have I got them all right?"

He said, "Including this time?"

I said, "Yeah."

He smiled and said, "This time."

I was stunned. They were so easy, yet I hadn't been able to get them all right. It was about that time the doctor was walking up to us and had Megan, Preslie, and Payten in tow.

He said, "You look great today."

I said, "I feel great today."

The doctor said, "Do you know who these people are?"

I said, "Yes," and pointed at Meg and said, "That's my sister Gertrude." I pointed at Payten. "That's my sister Henrietta." I pointed at Preslie as the smiles were fading from their faces. "That's my girl Preslie." Everyone's face had the "Wait, what?" look. Then I said, pointing at Meg, "That's my wife, Meg, my girl Payten, and my girl Preslie!"

I tell everyone that walking with Graham that day was like walking out of a dense fog back into the open. For me, that is when I felt like I was back in the moment for good. I still had my moments but spent the vast majority of my time in the present after that. The funk was gone. My whole day, when I look back on it, was leading up to that moment, and you could see there was a breakthrough coming based on how my day had been going. What a powerful moment for me. I still get emotional every time I think or talk about it. God is great, and he blessed me more than I deserved for sure and God gave me what I had asked for—another chance to see my family and tell them I love them!

We all laughed about my little prank, and I think Meg may have been a little skeptical if I was really joking or not, but it was real. I felt like me again. We all made our way back to my room. After that, the talk about my discharge and rehab really picked up some steam. They were saying that I most likely would be transferred the next day as long as they still had a bed for me.

I would be going to St. Luke's Rehab Center, which was just down the street, a short way from Sacred Heart. The administrators got back with us and let us know that St. Luke's did indeed have an open bed for me, and I was to be discharged from the hospital and admitted to St. Luke's at noon the next day, which ended up being 1:00 p.m. My new casa would be room 231 at St. Luke's.

As excited as I was to be discharged and off to the rehab center, I was also a little sad because the girls were going to be going home in the morning. I used their departure to help me focus on getting well as fast as I could so I could see them, and we all would be together again as soon as possible.

CHAPTER 21

The next morning, October 2, I got up and got dressed in street clothes. My sisters were there to see me. I got my picture taken with the girls, and they took pictures of Megan and me. Preslie and Payten were off to the airport, and I was in the process of getting discharged. Meg was in the process of gathering up what stuff I had at the hospital and her stuff at her hotel room because we were going to be roomies at the rehab center for the remainder of my time in Spokane. It was okay to have a family member stay in your room, so they were going to put another bed in the room for her.

For whatever reason, Meg wasn't allowed to ride with me to the rehab center. It was two or three blocks. They loaded me and my stuff up and took me to St. Luke's. Meg got there shortly after I did, and we began the process of getting me admitted there.

They helped us get everything to the room. They didn't have Meg's bed in there yet, but when they brought it, you could see right away it didn't look very comfortable at all, and after the first night, I'm sure Meg could confirm that it wasn't!

We were settled into our new digs, and it was nice to be present again after being gone for a bit. We had contact with my therapists, and I would be having physical, speech, and occupational therapies daily. I was about to be a very busy guy.

The second day in rehab was going to be an aha moment for me right off the bat! After Meg and I got up, the nurse came in and asked me, "Would you like to take a shower?"

I wasted no time in taking up that offer. It had been a while, and I was excited to have one.

The nurse went into the bathroom and came back out a minute later and said, "You're all set. I put a bench in the shower for you with a towel on it. The water is running. If it's too hot, turn the handle to the left. Take your time and enjoy it."

I went into the bathroom, shut the door, went to the sink to brush my teeth. When I got in front of the mirror, I just stood there staring at myself.

I had taken my pajamas off when I entered the bathroom and was startled at my appearance! I started to cry and thought, *What in the world happened? What have I been through?* As crazy as it sounds, I could hardly believe my eyes!

I could see my shunt, and I thought that I must have fallen on the way out and busted up my skull. My eyes were sunken into my head with dark rings under them. I had three different lengths of hair on my head going from bare skin where my shunt was placed, to buzzed where my incision was, to long on top of my head and the left side. I had a scar on the right side of my belly button where they had hooked my shunt into my digestive system, but the most startling thing was my weight! I had lost a massive amount of weight! I weighed 236 pounds before I left for Montana. Now my weight was at 202 pounds! I had the scar from my shunt on my head, and when I turned my head, I could see the void in the back left side of my head from the surgery.

I thought, *Man I'm a mess!* Then I thought, *God spared me. I'm going to get myself together and enjoy this shower and bust my butt to get better and out of here and get on with my life.* I thanked God for sparing me and told him, *I remember the deal we made on the mountain that day. You kept up your end of it, and I promise I will keep mine!*

I sat there in that shower with the water hitting me for a long time until I was good and puckered up and decided to get out. When I got out and dried off, I had another long look at myself. I still couldn't believe how I looked. Quite a sight for sure! I now had a full beard that needed to go, so I spent some time with my razor and worked on it till it was gone. It was an improvement for sure. When I put my clothes on, they just hung on me.

I opened the bathroom door and was in the process of putting my shirt on when I asked Meg, "How long have I been in the hospital?"

She said, "Hmm, I guess it will be heading into a month here pretty soon. Why?"

I said, "A month!"

She said, "Yeah, how long did you think you were in here?"

I said, "Five days!"

She said, "Five days?"

I said, "Yeah, I thought I had only been here for about five days."

Meg said, "No, I can tell you it's way more than five days!"

I'm sure for her it seemed like an eternity waiting to see what the outcome was going to be. God bless her, and how lucky I am to have her.

I didn't realize what a battle I had been in for my life. Now that I was in the moment and could actually comprehend what I looked like, my appearance boggled my mind.

Karen and Bonnie showed up, and I had to go to my physical therapy session. I spent time going up and down a set of steps that went up three steps to a platform and then back down three steps on the other side. I can say my balance was still pretty whacked, and it was a good thing there were handrails on the steps! After that, I bounced a giant ball off the wall overhead for a while. Then on to balance drills. They had me stand on one foot with the other foot extended out in front of me. Then they would have me stand on one foot with my other foot on my shin. Then I would walk around the perimeter of the room. I know it doesn't sound like much, but I was exhausted!

When I got back to the room, Meg, Karen, and Bonnie asked me if I wanted to go out for pizza for dinner. It sounded good to me, and we got ready and headed out. Karen and Bonnie had driven over, so they had a car for us to go in. I wasn't sure how that was going to go. I had a constant headache, and the car ride might be too much for my neck and head bouncing around and going around corners in the car, but I was about to find out. I had a stocking hat to wear. It was cold out, and the hat hurt my head on the back where the incision was, but I dealt with it.

We ended up going to a wood-fired oven pizza place. It smelled great when we got out of the car, and I was hopeful it would taste as good as it smelled. We got inside and were seated. My headache had gone up a notch on the way there, but it didn't hurt enough to make me want to go back to the room. We ordered two pizzas, one with everything and one with brussels sprouts on it with a zesty cheese. Not my type of pizza, but I did try a slice, and it was okay. After not eating for weeks, I felt like I was gorging myself. The pizza tasted so good. I ended up eating three slices. I was stuffed!

I was taking in the moment of just sitting with my wife and my sisters, such a simple thing taken for granted by myself for years but appreciated so much now. We always hear "be thankful for what, and who you have"! I always thought I was a person who was thankful, but I don't believe until this happened that I really got it. When you have an in-your-face moment where your mortality may be at hand, and you're sure there's no way you're getting out of it, then you do! That will make you realize how precious life is. I don't think that I truly appreciated what and who God had given to me in my life, but it was crystal clear now. I have always told my family that I love them, but now I tell my family and my friends how much I love them and always do. Don't ever miss the chance to tell someone you love them, and they matter to you, or you may miss your chance forever!

We have all had loved ones pass on around us, and when you're young, you never think about one day it's going to be you, but that day is out there for all of us. We don't know which one it is, but it is there, and it's coming. Don't have regrets. Life is short and can be gone in the blink of an eye. Enjoy life and those who God has placed in your life. Money is necessary but not the most important thing by far. Faith, family, and friends are what really matter in life. All the money in the world won't bring you true inner happiness or buy you another minute on this earth.

We made our way back to the rehab center, and my sisters parted company with us there. They had a place they rented for the night and were going there. Today had been a great day. I was tired, and I'm sure Meg was too. We got in our beds, watched TV for a short time, turned it off, and fell fast asleep.

CHAPTER 22

The next day was going to be a busy day! I had all three of my therapies today. A pretty big workload for a guy who hadn't done much for the last month. I was ready for the challenge and to put forth the effort and work needed to get me back to the best me I could get back to, whatever that was going to be so I could get back home and on with my life.

I have to say the people I was dealing with that do therapy for a living are fantastic at what they do. At physical therapy, we worked on my balance again and my neck strength. My surgery had left a pretty good size void in the back left side of my head and neck. We also worked on my overall strength and motor skills.

Speech therapy has very little to do with speech and can make you think, *Why am I doing this? I can talk fine.* In speech therapy, we were working on my multitasking, organizational skills, time management, planning, and things of that nature—all things that would help me when I would go back to work. I struggled the most in this therapy which was hard for me to understand because in my job, that is what I do and have done for decades. It had always been easy for me until now!

Occupational therapy was about following directions and life skills. Today, I was given a list of places located in the facility and had to find my way to each of them, a scavenger hunt of sorts. As simple of a task as that was, it helped to build my confidence back up in myself and that I was going to be okay at the end of all of this.

On the day of my injury, when we arrived at St. Pat's Hospital in Missoula, I remember the doctor saying to me in the ER after the

CT scan, "With the severity of the injury, the fact you were able to walk out of there, and you're still as functional as you are at the level you are, I would put the chances of all that at less than 1 percent! You should have fallen over dead."

There were so many things that happened that day and the days since that I shouldn't have been able to do but did, along with all of the things that could have stopped us from getting me to help but didn't. All I can say is how great God is and how fortunate I was to receive such great care at every level from St. Pat's to Life Flight, to Scared Heart, and now St. Luke's, all of my family and friends. All of that helped to drive me in my recovery because I didn't want everyone's efforts and prayers to be in vain because I chose not to work at my recovery as hard as they all had worked to put me in a position to get back to normal.

Back to my occupational therapy session. I did one other task today. I drove a driving simulator. I was thinking to myself, *Oh, I get to play video games for a while. Nice way to use up some time.* I started out in a very simple driving situation. I was on a country road driving and came up on a stop sign for me. As I continued to drive, I could tell I was getting closer to a town, and the distractions were continuing to increase. I was doing well in all of the situations and was now driving in town when two kids walked out from between two parked cars. I saw them in plenty of time, and the simulator seemed to accelerate as I was applying the brakes! *Bam*, and just like that I'm guilty of double manslaughter! Driving while impaired!

The therapist said, "Oh, that's not good!"

I said, "The machine accelerated after I took my foot off of the gas and applied the brake."

She said, "That's not possible!"

I said, "If I was driving in my truck for real, those kids would still be alive!"

Anyhow, we never could come to an agreement on that one, but those were the only two fatalities caused by me during my rehab. It had been a good day, and I felt like I had made good progress and went back to my room.

When I got back to my room, I got a phone call from a long-time friend and former roommate from when I was young and lived in Missoula, Montana—Dave. As we were talking, I found out he had actually come to see me in the hospital once already. We were roommates in the early '80s, and he had since relocated to Spokane from Missoula during that time.

Chuck had called him and told him what had happened to me and thought it would be good for me if he came to visit. I guess during the first visit, we did quite a bit of storytelling and laughed it up, but I didn't remember any of it! I asked him if he would be willing to come and see me again so I could remember it. Dave said he would, and it would be sometime soon. I was so happy he was willing to come and see me again.

I had been at a therapy session and was on my way back to my room. When I got there and opened the door, there was Dave! Not only was Dave there, but he brought his daughter Kylie with him. We got to visit for a while and revisited some great times we had in the past and laughed quite a bit along the way too. Dave had to pick his son Kaden up, and it was time for him to go get him. It was great to see him and meet Kylie. I wish I could have met Kaden too. Maybe next time.

I told Dave, "I love you, and you're like a brother to me."

We had a hug, and they were on their way. It's too bad that so many times, it takes things like what happened to me to get people back together, but it was awesome to see him after so long. I have, as Dave said, "much love" for him.

The days were ticking away, and you could tell I was getting stronger in all areas of my therapy. Talk of my departure and trip home was picking up steam, and I can tell you I was ready to go! It seemed like it had been forever and a day since I had been home. We were given a discharge date of October 9. What a great day it was when I heard those words. I was still doing therapy daily. That day in occupational therapy, I made brownies. Not a bad thing! I must say I knocked it out of the park following the directions because they were fantastic. I left most of them there but did take a few for me and Meg to snack on later.

121

With all of the talk about discharge, I asked Meg, "Where is my hunting stuff at?"

She said, "It's at Charlie's place."

I called him and told him what was going on and what date they were going to discharge me. Chuck was happy I finally had got to that point and said he would drive over and bring my stuff before then and to say goodbye.

When he brought over my stuff, we were visiting, and he asked me, "Do you remember when Kari came over with me to see you? Kari is Chuck's daughter."

I thought about it and we talked about it and I told him, "I have vague memories of that."

Chuck and Kari had come over to see me, and when they got to my room with Meg, they wanted to see if I would know who she was if she just walked in by herself.

So I was lying on my bed. Chuck and Meg were outside the room, and Kari came breezing in and said, "Hey, Kelley boy!"

She has called me that since she was little. There was another friend who was a girl and her name was Kelly, and Kari called her Kelly girl! Kari walked across the room and as I watched her, I was thinking to myself, *That's weird. What's she doing here?* Then Chuck and Meg walked in laughing.

When Kari had come in, she had a balloon that was shaped like a whale that said, "Get whale soon!" I can also remember that Kari was giving me the business big time. I don't remember how I handled it, but Kari told me I handled it well, and my sense of humor was intact during the time they were there. Good to know I took it so well when something like changing the channel on the TV was met with an outburst before. So I guess I remembered the visit; it just needed some prompting.

While Chuck was there, we talked about the day everything happened again, and my accounts of what happened were good up to the point when the Life Flight medic put the second syringe of medicine in my IV. After that, things were fuzzy for me.

Chuck told me my actions that day were "a great show of intestinal fortitude."

I told him, "I just wanted to see Meg and the girls again, and I was scared that wasn't going to happen."

Chuck hung out for a while. The weather was forecast to get bad, and it had already started when he was driving over to Spokane. So with two mountain passes to go over on the way home, he made the decision to head out. We shook hands and hugged each other. I told him thanks for everything he had done for me and how much it meant to me and how much I appreciated it.

His response was, "Would you have done any less for me?"

I said, "No."

Great guy, great friend. I love him to death. Chuck went on his way home.

With my upcoming discharge, there was a lot to do. Meg was busy on the phone talking to people about one thing and another, like my discharge, therapy for me when we got home, where therapy would be, and how we would be getting home. As she was talking about how we would be getting home, I kept hearing her saying things about taking a train. I was thinking, *Why in the world would we be taking a train home?*

I said, "I don't want to take a train home. I want to fly. Taking a train will take forever, and I just want to get home as fast as possible." So while Meg was on the phone writing stuff down and talking, I was giving her the business like a little kid! "Meg, why are we even talking about taking a train? I don't want to take a train. I want to fly. You're saying four days to get home by train. I want to be home as fast as possible!" I went on and on while she's on the phone. Then she gave me that look, the one that says, "Would you shut your pie-hole for a minute and let me finish and get off the phone," with her finger up, index finger that is! I sat there like a little kid pouting till she finished.

Then I started right back up with the same battery of questions, until she stopped me in midsentence when I heard her say, "You have another aneurysm in your brain, and they are concerned it may pop if you fly!"

I asked her where it was. She said she thought it was in my forehead because that's where the doctor pointed when she had asked him the same question. I felt gutshot to hear that. Meg said the doctor was going to let her know if I could fly or not. She said the doctor said the aneurysm was small but could still rupture in flight.

"If you can't fly, we will have to take the train home, and that will take four days."

There was also concern over my artery in my groin. They had been in there so many times in the last month and were using collagen plugs to seal the site which could be compromised if I flew too. I was dreading the thought of taking a train. My head was still killing me, and the thought of rocking on a train for four days would be utter misery, but if that's what we needed to do, that's what we would do. I would have to deal with it.

The word finally came back, and Dr. Carlson thought it would be okay for me to fly. Thank you, God! I wasn't sure how my head would feel flying, but I would be home the same day, and I liked the sound of that. The next day would be my last in the rehab center, and we would be flying home the day after that.

Meg had been in contact with the airlines, and they were going to honor both of our tickets to get us home and had me set up with wheelchair service from the front door to my seat. It was great they were so helpful in getting us home and honoring our tickets. Meg had explained our situation to them, and they wanted to help.

I want to share another random act of kindness that happened to Meg after she was in Spokane. One night, she went to the Olive Garden for dinner. It was on Newport Highway. Her server that night was Angela! Angela asked Meg where she was from and what brought her in that night. Meg told her the story about why she was there. After Meg was done eating, Angela brought her the check, and on the back of it she wrote,

> We took care of your bill tonight. Thank you for coming in! Please stay strong. I am praying for you all!
>
> Angela

Meg kept that receipt, and we still have it. What a beautiful thing to do and what a beautiful message she wrote. I don't know if Angela still works for the Olive Garden or not, but they are blessed to have someone like that on their team. That random act of kindness meant a lot to Meg, and it does to me too. There are good people no matter where you go, with big hearts.

The next day, my therapy was set up. I would have all three therapies even though it was my last day there. For my OT, the therapist set up a board game for the session. It was me and three other guys. I don't recall two of the guys' names but the third one; his name was Del! I don't know what had happened to him, but based on his appearance, I thought he was in some sort of accident. He was missing the lower part of one leg, so he was in a wheelchair, and he had a bandage on one arm too. Del spent most of his time in his wheelchair, in the wheelie position! Another note on Del; he didn't follow directions very well!

The game we were playing was you moved around the board and scored points. We were all tasked with keeping track of our *own score* in our heads. No one was to help anyone else with their score. I will say Del's math skills were on point! As I said, we were all to do the math in our heads. The other two guys were older than me, and Del was younger. We three older guys all had brain injuries; Del didn't, so every time one of us went, and we were busy adding up our score in our heads, Del already had it figured out and would just blurt it out.

The therapist corrected Del the first couple of times in a very nice tone and reminded him that "this is to help everyone get better, and you need to stay quiet and give the others time to work it out on their own."

Del said he would. The next roll of the dice, Del called out the answer again time after time. I think the other two guys were getting annoyed by Del. I'm not sure why I wasn't, maybe because I was losing, but I couldn't stop laughing at his refusal to follow the rules. Del looked like a cat ready to pounce on a mouse as soon as one of us would pick up the dice to roll. Del had a continuous smirk on his face along with a look of anticipation, waiting for the dice to settle so he could yell out the answer first. I know our therapist had enough, and finally, with Del's refusal to play by her rules, she ended the game. I will never forget the look on Del's face when she ended the game. He looked right at me with a smile from ear to ear, popped a wheelie, and wheeled himself out of the room!

I went back to the room, got a shower, and got dressed. Today in physical therapy, we were going out in public to see how I handled being around large groups of people with a lot of stimulation going on around me. The therapist, Meg, and I all got in the van and went for a ride. We rode around for a while, and she asked how I was doing. I told her I was fine. Meg suggested we go to a store to see how I handled that, and she wanted to see if she could find me one of those travel pillows for my neck. The therapist thought that was a great idea, and off to the store we went. Once there, we all went in and walked all over the place looking at stuff! Meg did find one of those pillows and bought it for me for the trip. I wasn't sure I would use it, but at least I had it if I needed it. I handled the store fine, but my head and neck were getting sore, and she said we needed to go, so we checked out and left.

Once we got back to the center and up to our room, Meg and I began wrapping up the packing process, except for what we would need in the morning. Our flight left at 6:00 a.m. That meant we needed to be up between three and four to give us enough time to get ready, get to the airport, check in, and to our gate. We got in our beds and shut the lights off. I had a terrible time falling asleep. There was so much racing through my head. I was extremely excited about going home but still had concerns about the flight and my other aneurysm. Then there were my head and neck issues and wondering how they would feel after today's outing and how the flight may affect them and possibly make the pain worse than it already was. Then on to another thing on my mind, the thoughts of having to get my other aneurysm fixed at some point. Would I be able to go back to work and do my job? Needless to say, I didn't get much sleep. The alarm went off, and I woke up with more pain than usual! Meg could tell right away I wasn't having a good morning.

CHAPTER 23

We got ready and loaded up our stuff in the car that was to take us to the airport and set out for the airport. I could feel my headache getting worse the closer we got to the airport. I was surprised at how busy the airport was when we arrived there, it being so early in the morning. This was going to be a notch up from yesterday's outing for sure. We got inside the terminal. Once inside, they got me in a wheelchair right away, so that was nice. We got checked in and to our gate. Once there, they let us know we would be getting on first which was nice, but I wasn't sure about sitting there waiting for everyone else to get on. I found the airport situation to be stressful and confusing at the same time. My headache was raging, and I just wanted the whole ordeal to be over. Meg gave me something for my headache and a drink of water to wash them down. I had on my stocking hat, and it was making my incision area sore which was adding to my pain level. I didn't want to take it off. I was getting enough stares as it was.

It was finally time to board the plane. We made our way down the walkway to the plane. I got out of the chair, and we made our way to our seats. Of course, when I sat down in my seat, I hit my head on the overhead compartment. That felt great! Meg got my neck pillow and put it around my neck.

We were to fly to Minneapolis, then to Columbus after a short layover. Lucky for me, I'm like a kid in a car when I get on a plane. I fall asleep every time. Once everyone was boarded and all of the pre-flight stuff was done, we taxied out to the runway and took off. I fell asleep pretty quick after takeoff and woke up when I heard, "Prepare the cabin for landing."

When I had a minute to gather my thoughts, I could tell my headache had subsided, and now I just had my normal headache. That was great! I felt so much better, and after not sleeping, that nap gave me some much needed rest.

We landed and got off the plane last. We looked for a restroom and then went and found our gate for our next flight. Once we found the gate, we had some extra time and decided to get something to eat. We found a place that had seating outside in the terminal area and picked that because of the seating, and their fish looked pretty good. We both got the fish, and it was as good as it looked

After I ate, I felt even better, and knowing that one short flight, and I'd be home had me feeling pretty darn good everything considered. As we made our way back to our gate, the thought of sleeping in my own bed was in my head big time. I was pretty excited about that happening. Once we got to our gate, we didn't have long to wait, and we were boarding the plane. Once the plane got into the air, I didn't fall asleep this time. I did have my eyes shut, but I was too excited to sleep.

I asked Meg, "How are we going to get home from the airport?"

She said, "Stu and Betty are going to pick us up."

Stu and Betty are our next-door neighbors, a true blessing to have them living next to us. We enjoy their company, and as neighbors, we are all willing to help each other out whenever there's a need. They are, as they say, "salt of the earth" people.

We were looking for a church to go to when we first moved to Grove City, and they invited us to go to church with them. They attend two different churches splitting their time between, the one they go to and the one their son Brad attends. The first time we went with them, we all went to the one Brad goes too. It's called Leave a Mark. Meg and I never made it to the other one because we both really enjoyed Leave a Mark. The motto there is "No Perfect People Allowed!" Fits us pretty well, we thought, and we have been attending church there ever since.

Stu had been taking care of things around the house with both of us out of state. He had been mowing the grass, moving the vehicles around so it looked like someone was around, and Meg and I knew they both were keeping a close eye on the place. Like I said, you couldn't ask for better neighbors. I was looking forward to seeing them.

Our plane touched down, and we taxied over to our gate. We got off last again, so we weren't holding anyone up. We got off the plane and made our way to the baggage claim. I was wondering where we would hook up with Betty and Stu, and as we were coming down the escalator, we could see them standing at the bottom of it looking up at us. There were smiles on all of our faces. We had our greetings and went to the baggage carousel that our bags would be coming to. The bags arrived, and Stu, and I grabbed the bags, and we were off to the truck. It was cold when we got outside, and there was a stiff wind blowing to make it feel even colder, but that's okay because it was a hometown cold, and it didn't bother me a bit.

Once in the truck, we talked about what happened. I told the shortened version up till I got to the hospital in Spokane, and Meg filled in the rest of the details from there. Betty and Stu both told me how lucky I was and how great God is.

Stu said, "We have been lifting you up in prayer!"

I thanked them for that and told them, "I could tell there were many prayers being said for me because I could feel them, and I appreciate them."

I told them as I was walking out after the aneurysm ruptured, I felt a calm come over me, and I felt God's presence was with me. I didn't feel alone. We made it to the development and made the last turn, and I could see the house! I was so relieved to know in mere seconds, I would be home. Just knowing that made me feel quite a bit better considering how I felt on that high mountain ridge the day of the injury. I thought I would never see the place again. Stu helped us with the bags, and we thanked them for everything they had done. They said they were happy to help, and it was a true miracle for sure.

Meg and I shut the door, and it was a done deal. We were home. Everyone's home has its own smell, and when I got my shoes and coat off, I sat down and found myself taking deep breaths through my nose, the same way I do in the mountains when the morning air warms up and shifts to an uphill draft pulling all of those beautiful smells of the mountains up for me to enjoy. It wasn't the same smell, but it was just as sweet to me. That moment was one that just felt so good and so satisfying. We watched a little TV. Then we went to bed. That was the best, crawling into my own bed after so long, another one of those little pleasures that is underappreciated by most of us for what a great feeling it really is.

CHAPTER 24

When I woke up the next morning, I went to the kitchen to get some morning brew going. While the coffee was brewing, I got out the papers the physical therapist had given me that had exercises on them for me to do at home to continue my recovery. I started out every day after my coffee, sitting on the edge of the couch. I would turn my head as far to the left as I could and hold it for a ten count, then to the right for a ten count. After that, I would hold my chin to my chest for a ten count, then look up, with my head as far back as possible, for another ten count. I would do ten, ten counts of each move. After that, I would lie on the floor and turn my head to the left and right with the side of my face on the floor or as close as I could get it for ten, ten counts each way. The steps in our house go up to a landing which are six steps, then turn and go up another eight to the second floor. When I first got home, I would walk up the six to the landing and turn around and go back down. I would do that, you guessed it, ten times. Then I would work on my balance drills they had me doing in the hospital, the one with my arms out, eyes shut, standing on one foot with the other out in front of me. Trying to get to a ten count was tough. I really struggled with this one. I would get to five or six and lose my balance every time. Meg would say, "Come on, hon, you can do better than that." Her saying that would make me try harder for sure. I normally would get to five or six, and a good run would be eight.

My head was still in constant pain, and my balance was off for sure on my right side. I was suffering continual onset of migraine headaches throughout the entire day. What I mean by that is for me through my entire day, it was one right after another all day, going through the process of losing my vision, with the start being a small spot that got bigger and bigger until I couldn't see anything other than a kaleidoscope effect. Then my vision would return, and then my headache would increase for an hour or so, then it would all start over, the same process all day long. For me, I was hoping it was a temporary thing and not my new reality for the rest of my life.

There is another thing that became routine for me too. Every day when I wake up in bed and open my eyes, I thank God for letting me start another day. Notice what I said there. I thank him for letting me start. There is still no guarantee I'm going to make it out of the day, but at least I get to start it. I thank him because at least I still get to be a husband, father, brother, son, friend, neighbor for another day. I used to take all of that for granted, but not anymore. The chance to be each one of those things is a blessing and should be thought of as such.

One other thing I know now is, the only thing in this world that has any true value is time! You may be thinking, *How so?* Here is how I see it now. If you have time, you can get anything you want, and I mean anything! If you're out of time, you're out of everything! So spend your time wisely on the things that really matter to you the most. Don't be a fool with your time. It means everything! If you're tired, take a nap. If you're lonely, get in touch with family and friends. We all need money, so go to work. We all need exercise, so get some on a regular basis. Take care of yourself so you can take care of yours!

While we were still in Spokane, Meg was scoping out neurosurgeons in Columbus. There were two that really stood out to her, and I got assigned to one in Columbus that wasn't either of the ones she liked. I asked Meg what it was about the one I got versus the other two because Meg was pretty set. She wanted me to see one of them, not the one I got.

She said, "The one you're assigned to only has ten years' experience, and both the other ones have over twenty years each. The reviews of the two she liked were between 4.7 to 5.0 out of 5 for both. The one I got was a 3.9 out of 5. Last but not least, Meg said the more letters they have after their name, the more knowledge and training they have. So in this example, Dr. Michael Smith, MD is just a regular doctor. Meg said the two she liked had half the alphabet behind the MD. It sounded logical to me. I had my first appointment coming up within the next week with my neurosurgeon, and by another unbelievable stroke of luck, I was contacted by Mt. Carmel, and I was reassigned to the doctor Meg liked the best! We never called or said anything about the other doctor. It just happened. I was assigned to Dr. Gewirtz, MD, FAANS, FACS. In looking at his reviews, the only knock against him were comments about his bedside manner. I don't care about bedside manner much. I was looking for a great surgeon who was going to shoot me straight, not a new friend, and he was the one Meg liked the most from her research.

I continued to do my stretches and balance work, trying to get stronger and progress as far back to normal as I could get. While I was doing my workouts, I started to add things to them to work my brain too. One of the things I added to my step workout was when I got up to the landing, I would turn to the right to come back down, and when I got to the bottom, I would turn to the left to go back up. I would also alternate which foot I started up the stairs with each trip. Seems simple enough, but not for me. I would turn the wrong way quite a bit of the time or continue to start up the stairs on the same foot every trip. Crazy when something is your main focus that you can't get it when you're specifically thinking about it, but that's the way it was.

The range of motion in my neck was getting better. I could see more and more of what was behind me when I was turning my head working on my neck motion. My appetite was coming back, and I had gained a few pounds back. Even though my appetite was coming back, eating wasn't that great. With my chronic salt wasting, I was put on a salt regimen when I was in the hospital, and everything I ate tasted salty to me! Ice cream, salty, and if what I was eating was salty like chips, forget it; they were too salty for me to eat. It tasted like I was just eating a handful of salt. I could still find plenty to eat. I just didn't need to use salt as I had in the past.

Another thing I was doing now for my balance is, I would stand in the kitchen by the closet wall. Meg and I had installed hardwood flooring the fall before, which turned out great by the way. I would stand by the closet with my hands on my hips and pick out a board out ahead of me that was more than a normal step away. I would step out and touch that board with my big toe, twenty reps per foot and three sets per foot. It was helping me out for sure combined with my other exercises they had given me to do.

I was still having issues with the exercise of standing on one foot with my arms out to the side and my eyes closed, still the right side giving me problems. My rupture was on the left back side of my brain and my right side had issues. Kind of like what they say; right-handed people use the left side of their brain, and left-handed people use the right side of theirs. So left-handed people are the only people in their right mind! Right?

So while I was doing this drill, Meg was giving me the business of, "Oh, come on, hon. You can do better than that!"

I said, "If you think it's so easy, come give it a try and show me what you got."

She accepted the challenge, got up, and moved to the open area of the floor in the living room. Meg put her arms out to the side, picked her foot up off the floor, closed her eyes, and I started to count out loud. I saw a bit of a waver around five or six, and when I got to seven or eight, she lost her balance and took a step.

I said, "Oh, come on, hon. You can do better than that!"

She laughed and said, "That's harder than it looks."

I said, "I know. You should see how hard it is after going through what I did!"

I was laughing too, but I love the fact she was always pushing me to get better, and I wanted to get better, not just for me but for the family so we as a family could have the best quality of time together going forward. We have always gone and done a lot of different things and had many different experiences, and I didn't want that to change because of me not being able to do it.

So I continued to work as hard as I could with the restrictions I had. I was only allowed to lift ten pounds at this point in my recovery because of the surgery. I had ten-pound dumbbells, and I was using them because I figured a little weight training was better than none.

I just want whoever is reading this to know that I know you either have or are going to try the balance thing, and I think you'll agree with me. It's not that easy to get to ten once, let alone every time! How about it?

Meg got a phone call from a couple of ladies we met when we moved to Columbus through softball. Our girls all played on the same travel and high school team. You get to meet a lot of great people through ball, and these two were a blast to hang out with.

They called to see if we were up for some company and if they could drop by. Meg asked me if I was up for it, and I was. They stopped by one afternoon. It was great to see them. The visit helped to break up my daily routine I was getting into and a nice trip back to normal and to be able to interact with others. When Julie and Jamie arrived, I told them the story, and we talked about a variety of other things that were going on. The girls had purchased some gift cards, which really surprised and humbled us. It wasn't necessary, but it was greatly appreciated by both of us. It is always a pleasure to spend time with the two of them, and after visiting for a while, they were ready to head out. We thanked them for coming and for the gift cards, and they went on their way. I know we both enjoyed the visit very much.

When we were still in Spokane, they had set up an appointment for us with my doctor in Columbus. I needed to get my blood work done to see if I was still on track or if I needed any adjustments to my meds. Meg was on a leave of absence from work and would be going back soon, and I would be on my own with therapy looming on the horizon. One thing we wanted to ask the doctor was about my ability to drive based on my injury. With Meg going back to work I would need a way to get to my sessions. Meg had been doing all of the driving.

We arrived for my appointment, got checked in, and took a seat. We didn't have to wait long, and they took us back. They drew my blood, and we waited on the doctor. When the doctor came in, he gave me the once over, and he said he couldn't believe that I lived through that injury and that I didn't have any deficits. We told him

135

about our rapidly approaching situation with me needing to get from point A to point B and asked what my status for driving was given my injury.

He asked, "Did you ever lose consciousness or have a seizure?"

We told him, "No."

And he said, "You're okay to drive then!"

Meg and I looked at each other in total disbelief. We finished up the visit, and on the way to the car, I asked Meg "Do you want me to drive?" with a big smile on my face.

Her reply was "No!" with a look of disgust on her face.

I couldn't believe she said no! I'm not going to lie; I really didn't want to drive at this point myself, but it was nice to know if I absolutely had to, I could legally.

Once we got home, I changed my clothes and started my workout. I had recently kicked things up a notch with the workout. I was now climbing the entire staircase, fourteen steps in all, and was still focused on my turns one way, then the other, and starting with alternating my starting foot. You wouldn't think adding eight steps to the process would make much of a difference, but it did. By the third or fourth trip to the top of the stairs, I was gassed! I kept pushing myself because I had places to go and things to do. I was still using the dumbbells, five and ten pounders, and had added a couple more lifts to my routine. I also started to pick up some of the chores around the house to help Meg out and keep myself moving.

We were notified that our first appointment with Dr. Gewirtz was set up, and I was looking forward to meeting him and seeing what he had to say about my other aneurysm. They had sent him my medical records and a disc of my injury and the repair done by Dr. Carlson. His office was on the northeast side of Columbus, about forty-five minutes away from the house, and on the day of the appointment, Meg drove us up there. When we checked in, I had to fill out the usual paperwork. Once done with that, I took a seat and was looking around the waiting room. It was big, and it was full. I could see there were people with varying levels of ability in the waiting room. Most of us had some visible sign on our heads that there had been some sort of issue.

We were finally called back. They got my weight, 212 pounds fully clothed with my coat and shoes on. Not bad. I could tell I had gained a little weight. The doctor's assistant came in and asked me several questions about my injury and my progress in my recovery. She took some notes and told us that the doctor would be in shortly.

The doctor came in, and we had a small introduction, then he asked me more questions about my injury and what had happened. He said, "So you're here to get your other aneurysm taken care of?"

We said, "Yes," and asked if he could tell us where it was located because Dr. Carlson had just motioned toward his forehead with his finger when Meg had asked him where it was.

Dr. Gewirtz said, "I want to be sure of its location, based on the size of it noted by Dr. Carlson as two millimeters." He said he was going to set me up for an angiogram to pinpoint its location. He also said, "I don't know who this Dr. Carlson is, but I can say in looking at how he finished off the artery, it was masterful work!"

That was it for Meg and me. We knew what Dr. Carlson's reputation was, and if Dr. Gewirtz, not knowing anything about Dr. Carlson, recognized his work as masterful, then he was the right guy! The way I saw it was he could either recognize it and do it himself, or he could recognize it and couldn't do it himself, but I was going with my first theory, and at that point, he had my total confidence.

I can also say that Dr. Gewirtz is a man of few words. He is very direct and doesn't sugarcoat anything. He wants you to understand every word he is saying so there is no miscommunication about what is going on or what is going to be going on. He had us stop by the front desk after the meeting to set up the angiogram and a follow-up appointment after the angiogram for the findings of the test.

Once we got to the car, I asked Meg, "Well what do you think?"

She said, "Well, he is a man of few words, but I like him. I think he's the right guy for the job."

I agreed, and we headed home. And no, I didn't drive!

CHAPTER 25

I want to share with you one of the reasons I'm writing this book. I grew up with very little contact with my dad. Since then, we now have a relationship I think we both are satisfied with. Before my aneurysm ruptured, my dad had been diagnosed with an aneurysm in his brain as well as one on the artery to his stomach. The aneurysm in his brain is located in the lower left back part of his brain on the artery in the exact same location as mine was!

We know this because he had gone to Spokane to Sacred Heart Hospital to have it "coiled," which is a procedure to render an aneurysm harmless. They go in your groin up into your brain through your arterial system, then put a very fine wire coil into the aneurysm that fills it up. A blood clot then forms over the aneurysm and seals it off rendering it harmless. His aneurysm was found after an angiogram that was performed before my rupture occurred. Dr. Carlson was the doctor assigned to him. After my accident and his coil had been performed, they met for a follow-up, and my dad said something to Dr. Carlson about me, and he recalled my injury. Dr. Carlson had referred my dad to another doctor who specialized in coiling, and that doctor did indeed do the coil on my dad's aneurysm. He went to the hospital, they did the procedure, and he spent the night in the hospital and went home the next day.

Here's the point. I asked if aneurysms were hereditary. I was told not always, but they can be. Based on that and the fact we both had an aneurysm in the exact same spot on the artery in the lower left back side of our brains, I'm sure they can be. If my dad knew they could be hereditary and had let all of us, meaning me and my siblings, know, we could have gone and got checked out head to toe. If one was found, we could then get it fixed without having to go through what I did. Since that time, we have had both of our daughters checked, and they are both fine at this time. They will go every five years from now on. My sister Linda was checked, and she was found to have an aneurysm in her brain too. It is small, and they are going to monitor it going forward, until it needs to be taken care of.

My advice: If you have had a mother, father, grandmother, grandfather, who has had or has passed away from an aneurysm, go to your doctor and get a scan set up from head to toe to see if you have one. If you do, you can get it taken care of and not have to put yourself at risk of what can happen if it ruptures. It will give you peace of mind. It will cost you some money, but it is money well spent that may just buy you extra time with your loved ones!

In our lives, we meet people who we have special relationships with. Some we meet later in life, and some we meet when we are kids. In my life, I met my brother from another mother in kindergarten. We have been friends ever since. There was a period of time when, after we graduated from high school, we lost contact for years, but when we reconnected, it was as if we had seen each other the day before.

After I got home from Spokane, my friend Randy, aka "Dolph," and two of his kids came out from Pennsylvania to see us. I think he wanted to see me with his own eyes to make sure I was okay. I know if he went through something like this, I would want to see him as soon as I could to make sure he was okay. When they arrived, we visited and shared stories of the events. Dolph and I have shared many laughs in our lifetime, and when Meg was sharing stories of some of my moments in the hospital, we shared some more. Dolph and I as well as several of my other friends tell each other "I love you" regularly.

Growing up, Dolph's family included me in many things in their lives that I wouldn't have experienced on my own. His dad, Ed, was a mentor to me and a good father figure who never missed an opportunity to correct me when I needed some tweaking. I called Dolph's mom, Mom when we were kids and still consider her to be a mom to me to this day. She is an amazing woman and a great role model.

When I was about eleven or twelve, I got invited to go to Cedar Point with them. They went every year and they could invite a friend to go and it was my turn. I couldn't believe it. Cedar Point is called the roller coaster capital of the world, and it is in my opinion. I got to tag along on hunting trips and help out with projects. We spent the night countless times as kids at each other's house, ate dinner with them, went to church. They made me feel welcome and comfortable, which I still feel to this day. Dolph and the kids spent a couple of days with us, then headed back to the hills of Pennsylvania. It's nice to know that someone cares that much to make the four-hour drive to check on you and let you know you're loved!

The date for the angiogram was set and fast approaching, and I was having some anxiety over it. The reason for that is, I was hit by a car when I was on my motorcycle riding home from work in the early eighties, and my left leg got beat up pretty bad. I have had a few surgeries on that leg for vascular issues since then and have had angiograms done before the surgeries. They went in my right groin area up to my heart and made a right turn and down to my left leg. Once they were there, they pumped dye into my vascular system to get a more defined look at any issues I had in my leg. When they pumped the dye in my leg, it hurt quite a bit. I consider myself to have a pretty good pain threshold, and I was surprised at how uncomfortable it was. The thought of having that done in my already aching head made me wonder how bad that was going to hurt.

The day arrived, and Meg and I got to the hospital at 6:00 a.m. We signed in and went to the waiting area. Someone came out and got me right away. It was the first case of the day. They took me back and got me set up for the angiogram. I had an IV set up. The staff was awesome, and everyone was busy doing something for the test.

The cardiologist asked, "How are you doing?"

I told him, "I'm a bit nervous about the procedure because I'm not sure how bad it's going to hurt my head. I've had this done to my leg, and it was uncomfortable, so I'm just wondering how bad it's going to be in my head."

He said that he could understand that, and if he could do it with me out, he would, but he had to ask me questions, so I needed to be awake for the procedure. I told him I understand and would deal with it. He told me he could give me something to relax me a bit, and I accepted the offer. He shot a syringe into the IV and, after a few minutes, asked if I was feeling any better, and I was.

He said he was going to start and would be doing my angiogram in four sections, one of each lobe of my brain. He was going to start on the left front. He told me he was going to tell me before he injected the dye.

There was a giant screen to my left that would show what was going on, so I was keeping an eye on it to see if I could see the aneurysm myself, like I would know what I was looking for or where while looking out of the corner of my eye. The cardiologist told me he had accessed my brain and was going to inject the dye. I braced myself for the pain. I heard the click and could tell right away when it went in. It hurt pretty bad! He asked if I was okay, and I said I was but can tell you, based on that injection, I was really dreading when he did that in the back left lobe of my brain. He moved to the right frontal lobe next, did that. It was about the same as the left front, uncomfortable.

He said, "I'm going to the left back side next."

I was tense right away! I heard the click, and I can tell you this. I thought my head was going to explode! It was intense. I hadn't had any pain like that the day it happened. I had a flash of brightness, and as it was subsiding, I could see all of the veins inside my eye all lit up. They slowly faded, and the pain did also to the normal level of pain.

He asked, "You all right?"

And I said, "Yeah, that was intense!"

He said, "One more to go, then I'll look them over and see if we need to take anymore."

I figured with my luck, the only one that would need redone would be the left back!

He was gone for a short time and returned and said, "I think we're good to go!" Then he asked me who my doctor was, and I told

141

him. He said, "Oh man, that's the guy you want. He's the best. The worst cases from Ohio and the surrounding areas get sent to him!" Just a little reaffirming for me that I was in good hands.

Time was passing, and I had been home now for two weeks. I could tell I was making progress. I was outside one day, and Stu was out. We met up, and we were talking.

Stu said, "You're looking better, and your voice is getting stronger."

It felt good hearing that and knowing my efforts were paying off. Since my injury, when I get tired, my voice gets weak, almost to the point of losing it. That comment from Stu kept my fire burning and let me know the hard work was paying off and made me even more focused on getting as much back to where I was before the injury. At times, small words can have a big impact in our lives.

My first therapy session was coming up, and I knew I would have to drive myself there, so I made up my mind I would go for a short drive! I had been in my truck and noticed my tank was low, so I decided for my first drive I would go to the gas station and fill up. The gas station was about two miles from the house, so it seemed like a reasonable distance for a reasonable need. I'll just drive there, get gas, and come back home. I hopped in the truck, backed her out of the driveway, swung around and headed out. Driving in the neighborhood was a piece of cake. The speed limit is 25 mph. It was the middle of the work week and the middle of the day, so no one was around the neighborhood, so all was well. I got to the exit of the development, and the speed on that road is forty. It is a pretty busy road. I looked left, right, left, all clear, and pulled out. From there it is a straight shot down the road and a left onto the road the gas station is on.

I was rolling up to the stop sign on the road the gas station was on and just needed to turn left. The speed limit on that road is 55 mph. There was much more traffic now, and I could feel myself getting a little confused. People were stacking up behind me who were turning left too. I saw an opening coming, and when it got to me, I pulled out and hit the gas. Only a half mile to the gas station now. I got there, pulled off the road, and up to the pump. I got out, put the nozzle in, and while it was pumping the gas in, I cleaned the windshield. While I was doing that, the pump kicked off, and I went over and finished it up, but before I left, I went inside to buy a couple of lottery tickets. I thought that since one part of my Chinese zodiac came true, the other part could too. I posted the "Health" part in the front of the book just as you open it. My "Financial" part said, "You will gain great riches through gambling or the lottery." Hey, if one part could be so accurate, why not both?

I walked out, got in my truck, and pulled up to the exit for the station. It can be a challenge getting out of there. The road I came down to get to the station meets up to a major artery into Columbus right there at the intersection where the station is located. There is always heavy traffic there. It wasn't an issue getting off because I didn't have to cross traffic to get into the station, but now I needed to cross to get to the lane back toward my house. I was sitting there processing everything and saw my opening and hit the gas and accelerated down the road. The rest of the trip was easy peasy, and in no time, I was pulling into the driveway. I thought my first drive had gone well! I also knew when I drove to therapy, it was going to be a whole other ball game—three lanes of traffic madness going sixty-five miles per hour and up. My appointment was in Hilliard, fifteen miles away, a little different than my trip for gas. My plan for that trip was to follow my own advice I gave to Payten when she drove to school an hour away. Find your spot, stay in your lane, and maintain your speed. I find if you drive the posted speed limit on just about any road, you will find yourself with less traffic around you because most are going faster than the speed limit, and some are slower, but not many actually go the actual speed limit.

CHAPTER 26

The day of the appointment

I got up, had some coffee and an English muffin, took a shower, and left for the appointment. When I got in the truck, I put the address in the GPS of my phone and hit start. I looked at all of the routes it gave me, but based on traffic, they wouldn't get me there till late, so I headed for the chaos that 270 can be.

I was focused on my drive the whole way, so focused in fact that what only seemed like a few minutes had gone by, and it was telling me to get off. I was at my exit. I followed my plan, and it worked out well for me. I had very little traffic around me on the trip. The facility wasn't far from 270, and I made my way there with no issues.

To say I wasn't nervous about the drive would be a lie, but after I got there, my confidence level had gone up in my driving ability. I had a little bit of confusion during the trip but was able to work through it. I parked and went inside and got checked in, found a seat, and sat down.

My therapist's name was Ann. She came out and got me. We went back to her office, and once we were inside, she shut the door and sat at her desk. We talked about my whole situation—what had happened, how I was doing, and what my expectations were for myself.

I told Ann, "I want to get to 100 percent or as close to 100 percent as I can."

Ann did an evaluation on me, then took me over to see the occupational therapist. I met with her for a few minutes.

She said, "I have looked over your records, and based on our conversation, I don't think you need to be meeting with me." She released me at that time.

That made me happy! Now I would only have speech and physical therapy. I felt that speech therapy is what I was really needing to get me prepared to go back to work, and I was ready for the challenge.

Recovery time for my type of injury is six to twelve months. I was on a leave of absence from work, which was rapidly coming toward an end. The leave was for three months from the date it was approved. I needed to be ready to go back to work at that time or risk falling into a "Non-Job Protected" status. I would still be employed, but they would fill my job, and I would have to take whatever management position was open on whatever shift that may be. Most likely, it would be second shift or weekend day or nights. I also had the option to put in for an extension if needed. I wanted to be ready though because the extension could be denied.

My physical therapist's name was Josh. My first appointment with him wasn't for a few weeks yet, and with occupation canceled, Ann set me up to meet with her twice a week to start with and would adjust it later if we needed to.

Our niece Jenna is a speech therapist. She told me, "You'll become good friends with your speech therapist."

I said, "How do you know that?"

She replied, "I have seen relationships formed from people going through so much with their therapist that a friendship was formed and it continues on."

I figured she should know, so I took her word for it. I left the appointment and was optimistic I would be ready to return to work on time. Ann told me how each session would go in regard to how it would be laid out. I told her I was looking forward to our next meeting to see how I would do.

I continued my workouts at home. It was late fall now, and all of the leaves were falling from the trees at a good rate and needed to be cleaned up. So I worked that project into my workout. I don't rake anymore. I bought a blower. It is so much faster, and when you have a good tail wind blowing, you can move some leaves in a short time.

145

Stu was working, and my neighbor, Kevin, on the other side was working too, so I decided to do all three of our yards. I knew they could use the help because it was getting dark sooner, and I want to be a good neighbor. Plus no sense in just doing my yard and not theirs, then having the leaves from their yards blow into mine. I had the time to do all three, plus I was getting more workout time in. I would spend hours outside working on the leaves. It would wear me out, but I could also tell my endurance was getting better, and I know Stu and Kevin appreciated it. They are both hardworking men and I felt they could use a break and I could use the extra exercise.

A couple of days had passed, and it was time to go to my next appointment with Ann. I had been driving more and was feeling more confident about it, and the drive up to Hilliard went well.

I checked in, and Ann came right out for me. When we got to her office I could see there were tasks written on the white board and each had a time written by it.

She said, "During our session, when we get to the time that is written on the board on the clock, I want you to stop what you're doing and complete the task on the board, then go back to what you were working on."

Ann then gave me a sheet with four pictures on it to memorize. She told me to take my time and study the sheet, and when I felt like I had them memorized, to give her the sheet back. I looked at it for some time and felt like I had them logged in my data bank and gave the sheet back. Ann set it off to the side.

Ann then got another sheet out and told me, "The task here is I will read you four things from the sheet."

An example of what she would read to me are, "Coal, snow, wood, ice, which two will burn?" I would then tell her which ones. There were ten of these on a sheet. We started on doing the same items and I was really laser focused on getting them correct and I was nailing them.

I will say after a sheet and a half of those, it got hard to remember the four words she just read me, let alone which ones to pair up. I could tell my brain was getting fatigued. It was about this time I remembered the board and the tasks written on it! I thought, *Oh crap, the board!* When I turned around and looked at the board, I had already missed three of the time intervals and the task I was to do at those times. I was mad at myself for failing. I had been so focused on doing a good job, and I forgot about the total workload, which is what I need to be able to do to go back to work. My job is nothing but time management and prioritizing. Every day I do the same thing, but no two days are ever the same. I give Ann credit. She just sat there quietly reading the words to me, knowing I was missing my marks. She could have said something to me, but she knew that won't do me any good in the long run. That moment during that session gave me total respect for her and what she was doing to help me get better. It has got to be hard to sit there and watch someone fail, knowing it will be the best thing for them in the end.

I completed my three missed tasks, and we continued with the word sheets. Then about forty-five minutes into the session Ann reached over and picked up the sheet I had studied at the beginning of the session and said, "Okay, what are the four pictures on the sheet?"

I was sitting there thinking, *That is a great question. What are the four pictures on the sheet?* My brain was fried! I felt like I was in the ring with Mike Tyson, and he just launched the knockout punch right upside of my head!

Ann told me, "Take your time and think about it, as long as you need."

I ended up remembering three of the four pictures on the sheet. It was about that time my last time rolled around for my board task, and I completed it. I missed three out of five on that task.

I wasn't feeling too good about my first session with Ann. Then Ann did a recap of the session, and told me, "You did a good job with everything considering how much there was to do."

I can't say I felt the same but told her, "I'll do better at the next session. I promise you that!"

I got my coat and picked my broken pride up off the floor and walked out to my truck completely mentally exhausted, thinking, *Ought to be an interesting drive home with my brain a total mess.*

On the way home, my mind was racing thinking about my sessions and thoughts of *Am I going to be able to get to where I was before? Will I be able to do my job? What if I can't do my job? What am I going to do?* It was then that I thought to myself, *No matter what, God will give me what I need. He will make a way for me. He already had, how many times before, and he will do it again.* I decided not to worry about it anymore, but I did promise myself that in two days, when I went back, I wasn't going to do better; I was going to do much better.

When Meg got home from work, she asked, "Well how did it go?"

I told her, "In my opinion, not so good, but Ann said I did a good job."

Meg said, "I'll go with her impression."

Women, always sticking together! I let Meg know my concerns about being able to do my job.

She said, "That was your first session. Give it some time and see how it goes before you make up your mind about being able to do your job."

I told Meg I was going to do better in the next session.

During my first meeting with Ann, she had shared with me different techniques to help me remember things. I hadn't remembered to use any of them during the session. The first thing was simple, to just make a list of the things I needed to do. It seems simple, but I didn't think of it. The second technique was to categorize things, put like items together. The sheet she gave me to memorize at the start I could put them together, like animals, food, furniture, cars, weather, whatever they were. The third way was to make up a story and work it out using all of the pictures to make it up. So I was planning on using whatever I could this next time to do better and win the day!

At the next meeting, as soon as we got to Ann's office, she pointed out the board. I asked if she had a piece of paper I could have. She gave me one and asked if I needed a pen too.

I said, "No, I brought my own!"

I wrote down all of the tasks from the board and what time they needed to be done so I didn't have to look behind me. I set the paper where it was in my line of sight to prompt me. There were two more tasks this time than last time on the board. Ann handed me the sheet with the pictures, and it too had two more pictures on it than last time. After looking at the sheet, I decided to go with the story to be able to remember them. I made up my story and gave the sheet back to Ann. We talked about what was on the sheet, and then she set it aside. We once again started with the four words and which ones were alike. I was nailing those, and with my new sheet sitting in front of me, I was also hitting all of my timeline tasks.

My story was made up of these six words: *tent, lawnmower, bike, newspaper, kite*, and *light bulbs*, and it went like this! "I went camping in my tent. The grass around my camp was long and needed mowing, so I got out the lawnmower and mowed the grass. After that, I rode my bike into town to get a newspaper and some light bulbs. I noticed on the way into town it was windy so I also bought a kite to fly when I got back to camp." Amazing story to say the least, and I said I wasn't a writer.

When Ann did her summary at the end of the session, she said, "You did much better this time, not that you did bad the first time because you didn't. You did much better with the timeline and the pictures as well as the like items."

I was happy with my session and the improvements made from the first one. I was committed to keeping the improvements coming on a regular basis going forward.

CHAPTER 27

I had mentioned my new friend Mac earlier on. After we met at the bow range, Mac had invited me to hunt with him at his place. His house is about fifteen minutes from my house. I had been working my butt off in the hopes of getting back out hunting before the season was over but really before the rut was over. Ohio has a very long bow season. It runs from late September till almost the middle of February. There are two short gun seasons and a short four-day muzzleloader season, but the rest of the time, it is bow season only.

I recently had my weight limit moved up to twenty-five pounds. One day, while I was in the basement, I thought I would get my bow out and see if I could pull it back. I got my bow case down off the rack and set it on the workbench and opened it up. That was like opening up a time capsule! Once I opened it, I was standing there looking down at my bow lying in the bow case. It was still covered in dirt and dust from the mountain. My arrows were still equipped with the broadheads on them for hunting and one with the judo tip for shooting grouse. As I was looking at it all and taking it in, a flood of emotions came over me. The reality of the moment that had taken place the last time I saw my bow came rushing back, and it overwhelmed me, just how close I had come to my end, then the thoughts of everything I had been through since that day on the mountain and how far I had come since then! I never thought that opening that case was going to be such a powerful event, but it was, and I wasn't ready for that. It took me a few minutes to get myself back under control, and I picked my bow up out of the case.

I shoot my bow in the basement of my house. I could only shoot fourteen yards but good enough to work on my form. I took a broadhead off one of the arrows and put on a field point. They are what you use for practice. I stepped to the far wall across the basement from the target and hooked my release to the string and started to draw my bow. I had been home a month now and working on my body every day to get back to where I had been. As I pulled with everything I had, I got nowhere with my draw. I couldn't budge it at all.

I texted Mac and told him I couldn't even get any movement out of the draw. He sent back some things for me to try to help get my draw strength back. I put my bow back in the case and closed it back up and put it back on the shelf. I decided right then my goal was to get back to being able to shoot my bow and shoot it accurately and get back out hunting before the season was over.

Before I knew it, it was Tuesday again and time for my therapy again. Today, when I got to Ann's office, I could see she had added two more tasks to the board than the last session. I asked for a piece of paper, which she gave me. Then she gave me my sheet with the pictures which had eight pictures on it this time. After studying it for a few minutes, I decided I would use the like items method today. It made sense based on the pictures. I gave the sheet back, and we went right into the items sheets. She had more of those today too, which meant we would be going through them faster because the sessions are an hour; that's it. The word sheets had a new twist to them this time. Instead of them being like items, they were three words, and I had to put them in order. An example is she would say "June, April, May," and I had to say them back in the correct order, "April, May, June." Then there were ones like *street, tree, rain,* and I had to say them back in the correct alphabetical order—*rain, street, tree.* Much more thinking involved this time than the last. After two sheets, my brain was mush again.

After it was all said and done, I had missed one of my board tasks, and then she pulled the picture sheet out. She had to prompt me on two of the pictures to be able to recall them. I felt pretty good overall about the session given the extra workload. I have to say, with all of the extra stuff and mixing up my word sheets into a new format, I had only missed a couple of things out of everything we had done. Ann felt the session was a good one and, *I had done well!* There was progress being made, and I could see it for sure from where I had started. That being said, there was much room for improvement too.

My daily workouts were also progressing nicely. I was now doing the steps twenty times to the top and doing two steps at a time. I was still doing my turns and making far fewer mistakes than before. My balance was improving. I was making it to ten quite a bit now, and my range of motion in my neck was much better. I felt the motion was close to 100 percent, but I still had better motion turning to the right than the left. I had also started doing sit-ups and was up to fifty a day now, and with my increased weight limit, I could tell I was getting stronger.

I still couldn't pull my bow back yet but was shooting my recurve bow. I liked how it "stacked up" when I pulled it back and felt that was a faster path to being able to pull the compound bow back sooner. The recurve bow gets harder to pull the farther you pull it back, which would help strengthen the muscles needed to pull my compound back.

The two bows both come with their own style for shooting them. The recurve, you aim as you draw the bow, and when you get to full draw and hit your anchor point—which for me is the corner of my mouth—you let it go. When I say aim, there are no sights on the recurve bow. I use the tip of my arrow as a reference point, and from repetition of shooting, I know how the trajectory of the arrow is at different distances and use the arrow tip to determine how high or low it needs to be to get to my intended impact point on the target.

With the compound bow, you hook the release to the string, and as you draw the bow, the weight stacks up and then lets up at full draw, making it easier to hold and acquire your peep sight which you look through at your pins. You then position them on your intended target. Once you're settled there, then you pull the trigger on the release, and the arrow is on its way.

So I was shooting the recurve bow hoping it would get me to the point I could shoot the compound bow and get out hunting.

Worse-case scenario, I would just hunt with the recurve bow. I would give myself a twenty-yard limit if I hunted with it and stick to it. I can shoot farther with the compound and still be very accurate, but without the strength to pull it, it didn't matter.

After shooting the stick bow for a few weeks, my curiosity got the better of me, and I was looking at my bow case and went to get it off of the shelf. I took it over to the workbench and opened it and took it out. I hooked the release on my wrist, got an arrow out of the case, and stepped back to the far wall. I hooked the arrow to my string, then hooked my release to the loop and raised the bow up and started to draw.

I could tell right away I was going to get to full draw. I got to full draw and acquired my peep, then my sight pin, and settled the pin on the target and slowly started to add pressure to the trigger, with the pin hovering over the intended spot on the target. As the pressure on the trigger increased, in an instant, the release let go of the string, and the arrow was on its way and buried itself deep in the middle of the intended target! Success! I succeeded! I grabbed another arrow, put it on the string, and started to draw. Nothing doing. This was a one and done this time, but I knew now I could do it. I texted Mac and told him. He was happy for me but not quite as much as I was, I don't think. This was a big day and a big deal for me.

I had been talking to Dirsch. And if you were wondering what happened to him, Dirsch has his own business, and the day after my surgery when we were both to fly back home, he flew home to take care of his business and go back to work.

I had shared my inability to draw my bow back over the phone, and Dirsch was supportive and told me, "Keep working at it. You'll get there." I texted him and told him I got a shot off, and it flew true. And in true Dirsch fashion, he responded, "Perfect."

It was late October, and I got a package delivered to me here at the house. I was thinking, *I don't remember ordering anything.* And I was wondering what it could be. Once I got inside and got my glasses on, I could see that the package had been sent from Girard First United Methodist Church. This was the church we attended when we lived in Michigan. Dirsch and his wife, Courtney, as well as his entire family all attend church there too. That is how we ended up going there. I was pleasantly surprised and felt overwhelmed that they had sent something. I opened the box and found a note and a prayer blanket inside. The note said that they were still keeping me in their prayers. There was another sheet that told me about the prayer blanket. The church had made the blanket themselves for me. Knowing they took the time to do that for me was moving, and I greatly appreciated the blanket, note, and prayers. I know there was a small army of people from all over the country who were praying for me, and it meant the world to me to know that many people cared. When Megan got home from work, I showed her everything, and she was moved by the gesture as well.

The people that go to that church are just great down to earth, hardworking people, and the blanket was used that day after I got it. I did send a thank-you note back to the church but felt that it couldn't express how much everything was truly appreciated by us.

The first week of November is one of the best times to be in the woods to catch a mature buck up on their feet cruising in the daylight looking for love.

The first part of November is also when our wedding anniversary is, which is not a good day to be in the woods trying to take a deer, and I make sure I stick to that! I had been shooting my compound bow now and shooting well enough to go hunting. I had all of my gear ready to go and was set up to go hunting with Mac. It was the first Saturday of November. I had talked to Meg about it, and I'm sure she wasn't as excited about the thought of me going hunting as I was. Mac was a big reason she agreed to let me go. First, he had offered. Second, there was no way Meg would have let me go by myself in case something did happen.

I was so excited when my alarm went off. I thanked God for giving me the day and rolled out of the sack and got a pot of morning brew going. Then I was off to the basement to get all of my stuff hauled upstairs and to the front door. Then off to the shower for a quick shower. I, like many hunters, am very scent conscious when it comes to deer hunting and spend a lot of my preparation time making sure I have done my best to eliminate as much scent as possible.

The reality is, you can never get completely scent free, and the best thing you can do to stay undetected is stay downwind of where you think the deer will come from, keep the wind in your face, but every little bit helps if the wind gets fickle.

I loaded up after double-checking everything and drove to Mac's. He was in his garage getting all of his gear ready to go. We exchanged our usual greetings of derogatory name-calling and headed out.

We took his four wheeler because he was going to drop me off at a ladder stand. I was going to hunt on the edge of the field where a drainage ditch came into the woods. The deer like to run the ditches. Then he was going to his spot about eight hundred yards away across the road and field. He was going to use my buck decoy to help in getting a buck in if one showed up. Mac was looking for one specific buck, a big ten point he had named Nightshade. Mac was hunting off the ground, so that is why I suggested he use my decoy to keep the deer focused on it so he could get his bow drawn if the opportunity presented itself.

After Mac dropped me off I got up the ladder into the tree and secured myself off to the tree with my harness and lanyard. I pulled my bow and backpack up and got everything situated, put my release on my wrist, and nocked an arrow on my bow. Then I did as I said I would. I texted Meg and let her know I was safely up and in my stand and secured to the tree.

As I sat there in the waning darkness of another approaching day, I was filled with joy to be able to watch the sun come up as I had so many times before. It was a bit cold, but I welcomed it. Being cold is one of those things that let you know you're alive! As the light continued to grow, I could see deer to my left but couldn't make out much more than that, but one was chasing another around, and I was pretty sure it was a buck. I waited a bit longer until the light was good enough to see my pins and grunted in that direction.

As soon as I grunted, the deer stopped chasing the other deer, looked in my direction, and started my way at a steady trot. I was standing up, bow in hand, with my release hooked up. The wind was working in my favor as the deer approached. It's amazing how wild animals can pinpoint something after hearing it to within a couple yards after only hearing it one time. As the buck approached, I could see he wasn't mature and knew I wasn't going to shoot. That must be why he came right to me and stopped perfectly broadside at eleven yards. He looked around for about half a minute, then remembered his girlfriends who were moving out across the field in Mac's direction and ran over and joined them. Couldn't ask for a better start to the day than that. As far as I was concerned, my day was made. I could have cared less about what happened the rest of the day at that point.

I was using my binos and looking over Mac's way across the fields and could see the decoy, and every now and then, I could see Mac, but only if he moved. He was nestled up in a deadfall on the ground, and he blended in pretty good.

Bow hunting deer off the ground is intense when you have an encounter. The adrenaline pumps a little bit harder when you are eye to eye with your intended target. A little before eight, Mac sent me a text saying he had just shot the buck he was after. I was happy for him. He added that the encounter was way more intense than he expected, and the adrenaline rush was almost too much. He had tunnel vision, and his breathing was short and sporadic, making it hard to get settled on his target but was sure he had hit him well. Mac has only been hunting for a short time and is still learning every time he goes out. I'm sure it was quite a moment for him.

When you have the old adrenaline raging through your veins, it can be hard to remember things as they actually happened. Mac had put a fatal hit on the deer and, after some hard looking, was able to recover the buck. I had worked the trail with Mac until I was too fatigued, which didn't take long, then another guy came in and helped Mac finish up the trail. I went over the next day to get a look at old Lampshade, up close and personal.

Mac said, "What did you call him, Lampshade?"

I said, "Yeah, that's what you call him, isn't it?"

He started laughing and said, "No, I call him Nightshade."

We had a good laugh about that and still do to this day, but I can tell you, Lampshade hangs on the wall in his house next to Big John. I officially renamed the deer. It fit him better than Nightshade!

I don't know if any other hunter has had someone rename a big buck they were trying to kill after they killed it, but Mac did.

I got a couple of other hunts in that week and had my next appointment with Dr. Gewirtz coming up on the seventh to find out what the angiogram showed. Meg and I went to the appointment together.

CHAPTER 28

Meg left work early because she wanted to make sure of all of the information. I have a tendency to forget things and leave out critical details.

Dr. Gewirtz came in and looked me over, asked how I was doing.

I told him, "I'm doing well and working daily to get stronger and back to 100 percent."

We asked him about the aneurysm and when he was going to coil it, and where it was located. He said he knew where it was now.

I asked, "Is it behind my forehead?"

He said, "Well, kind of. If you put your finger on your forehead between your eyes and the other finger by the top but in front of your right ear, where those two lines intersect in your brain is where it is."

We both had this look of "Oh" on our faces, and then I asked, "When can you do the coil?"

Dr. Gewirtz said with some hesitation, "Well, it can't be coiled because of the shape of it. Most aneurysms are shaped like a berry hanging off a branch. This one is shaped like a wide spot in the road."

I was wondering what that meant for me, *Am I just going to live with it until it ruptured and took me out or what?*

Dr. Gewirtz said, "I'll have to go in and put a clip on it."

I remember thinking, *How is he going to do that through my groin?*

Then he said, while pointing with his finger on the right side of my head, "I'll make a three- or four-inch incision right here in a half-moon shape. I'll use a scope once the incision is made and move to the area while watching a monitor to guide the scope. Once I reach the area, I will place the clip, remove the tool, and then they will close you up."

I couldn't see my face, but I could feel all of the blood wash out if it. I had to be white as a marshmallow. I was thinking, *Did I survive the rupture to go through this, after my recovery was going so well, and I was starting to feel like myself again?* Who could know how it would go or how I would do with the doctor going into the middle of my brain, then back out? I was sure there is plenty of bad stuff that could happen during the process.

Dr. Gewirtz asked, "Do you have any questions?"

I did not. I was still trying to process what he had just said. Meg, on the other hand, did!

Meg asked, "Should he be hunting?"

Dr. Gewirtz said, "What kind of hunting?"

Meg replied, "Bow hunting."

The doctor asked me, "How many pounds is your bow?"

I said, "Sixty-four pounds"

He didn't even hesitate and said, "No, I don't think that's a good idea!"

Oh man, I was hot! I tried not to show it, but I don't think I pulled that off. I was also disappointed because that is one thing that made me feel normal, and that everything was going to be okay. I didn't say much on the way home, and once we were home, I went right to the basement and put all of my hunting stuff away for the year.

I told Mac, and he thought I was kidding at first, but after a minute, I was sure he could tell I wasn't kidding. I also told Mac they were going to have to cut my skull again and go to the middle of my brain to clip the aneurysm based on its shape. He, like me, couldn't believe it.

I told him I was worried that after everything that had happened up to this point, and that I was still okay, and now I had to put everything on the table literally and risk it all again so I could finally get on with my life spooked me big time. Mac gave me some words of encouragement, and we hung up.

Meg and I were hoping at least we could get the second surgery done before the end of the year for financial reasons and had asked Dr. Gewirtz's scheduler how things looked to make that happen. She wasn't optimistic that it would happen unless there was some sort of cancellation.

My therapy sessions were picking up. Now I had speech and physical therapy each time I went. I had speech first with Ann, then I would go to physical therapy with Josh right after with my brain in mush mode.

Josh did an evaluation on me and felt like I needed some extra work on my neck strength and mobility. He did say that he felt my overall condition was pretty good, so we would focus on my neck for the most part. He said to continue my at-home workout program and gave me more home workout exercises to add into my routine. Josh had me doing a lot of reaching-type exercises for my mobility, to the front, side, and above head. He had me using five- and ten-pound dumbbells when I was doing strength exercises and had cut and given me some bands of different resistance to take home so I could do the same exercises that I was doing at therapy.

My sessions with Ann had progressed. The board now had eight tasks with the times I was to do them on it. My sheets with the pictures to remember now had ten pictures on it. During the sessions, Ann would play music, and people were calling in to her office and knocking on the door and coming in and having conversations with her or not knocking at all. Sometimes they just barged right in and started talking. All of these distractions forced me to focus to keep my place on my task I was doing. It was confusing for sure, but that was what I would need to go back to work and be able to do my job to the level I needed to. Ann was giving me two or three sheets to take home with me after every session and bring back completed to the next session. Some of those sheets were a new type of sheet. They were sheets that made me use reason, based on vague clues, to get to the correct answer. I was needing quite a bit of help on a regular basis for these sheets. When I was at home, Meg would help me out when I got stuck.

Meg did say of the sheets, "They're hard for me, and I didn't have a brain injury."

It made me feel a little better knowing she thought they were hard too.

Thanksgiving was approaching. I was very excited because we were all going to be together again for the holiday. Preslie and Kam would be driving down from Michigan for a few days.

Kam is Preslie's fiancé. They have liked each other and been together since middle school. He was in eighth grade, and she was in seventh. They are both in their midtwenties now. Pretty uncommon it seems for nowadays. Payten would be home from school too. She was just an hour away, but she could be across the country it seems when we don't see her for a couple of months at a time. I was very much looking forward to us all being together and having the turkey meal. It is one of my favorites, and Meg does a great job with it! This is another one of those little things in life that can be overlooked as to what a special moment it truly is. I think we were all looking forward to it a little bit more this year than in the past knowing it almost didn't happen.

I had talked with Preslie about our family gatherings, and we both agreed that the time leading up to and during a family visit were the best because you're missing each other so much you couldn't wait to see each other and spend time. We also agreed that after the visit was over, and we all went our separate ways, it could be equally miserable because you didn't want to see them go. I found myself down for a day or two after we parted company, wishing it wasn't over so soon. I know this after my injury; you can't just say until next time, or we will do it when we get together again because there is no guarantee that it will happen. Anyone of us can be gone in the blink of an eye or the turning of a head, so make the most out of your time you have with each other. Get all of the hugs and kisses you can and tell others how much you love them. Don't leave anything to chance and have regrets over a missed opportunity you passed up.

As time was flying by with my recovery and my therapies, a couple of things had exposed themselves about the new me after my episode. First one was, with my head hurting all of the time, I hit my head on everything, almost daily it seemed. When I hit my head, it not only hurt my head; it hurt my neck too if I jammed my head

161

into something pretty hard. You would think that someone with part of their skull removed would be hyper aware of the possibility of running their head into things around them. Not so much for me. I find that when I am in a tight area, and I am focused on something in front of me, I totally don't remember that I am in tight quarters, and as soon as I get what I want or complete a task, I just stand up or back out while raising up and, bam. I hit my head getting in and out of vehicles that I never had an issue with before, no matter how big or small it is. I could be walking from one room to another in the house and forget something and turn around to go back into the room and get whatever it was I forgot and hit my head on the door that I had just walked by as I turned around. It was unbelievable and painful, but I just couldn't seem to prevent the occurrences from happening. To me, during those times, I had tunnel vision and lost awareness of things I knew were present.

The other thing that was going on and remains a strongly disputed subject had to do with my driving! Every time, and I mean every time, I drove somewhere with my wife, she would sit over there in the navigator's seat and be hanging onto the door or the "Oh, crap!" handle, gasping while I was driving, all the while telling me to "move over this way," motioning with her pointer finger her way. She constantly accused me after my injury of riding the center line every time I drove somewhere. I can't tell you how much time we have spent going back and forth on this subject, but it is way too much as far as I'm concerned. I have been driving my truck for years and know where my tires are in relation to the road.

I would say, "I'm going right down my lane."

She would retort, "No you're not. You're on the center line."

Then I would move over to the white line on the side of the road and ask, "Is this better?"

And she would say, "Yes."

To which, I would say, "I'm on the white line now."

It was exhausting!

My buddy Dolph and his mom stopped at our place for the night on their way to Kansas to see Dolph's brother Ed, and this topic came up. Dolph's dad had fluid on his brain too and had to have a shunt placed to help him with the issue. My buddy and his mother talked about how Big Ed did the same thing when he drove! Oh, good Lord, they both just validated Meg's belief. I had been betrayed by the two of them, and neither of them had even been for a ride with me to see for themselves, what the truth was. When they said that, Meg looked at me with that smug look people get when they know they're right, even though in this case she was not. We will have to agree to disagree in this case. I haven't changed anything about the way I drive, and she doesn't say anything anymore about me riding the line.

I brought it up to her, and she said, "That's because you don't do it anymore."

This is why a man should never, and I mean ever, argue with a woman. Oh yeah, and Dolph and his mom were both removed from the Christmas mailing list over this betrayal. That's just something I say to people. It didn't really happen!

It was now December, and I had a lot of things coming up, along with everything else I had going on already. I was to return to work after New Year's and still had my other surgery coming up. Christmas was coming, and I had shopping to do. I used to procrastinate big time on the shopping, and the reason I got proactive on it is because it is much easier to find what you want to buy for people before Christmas Eve! That is for the guys reading this and is your tip of the day, and it is a crazy good tip that may just help out a woman or two also!

My therapy sessions were going well, and at the previous session, I had discussed with Ann that the next session would be my last one before returning to work. This was because my insurance only pays for so many therapy sessions, and I had a few left. With me returning to work, it may be a good thing to bank a few; that way, if after I went back to work and needed help, I could go back to Ann and let her know what I was struggling with, and we could work on it.

The day came for my last session, and I had mixed feelings about it. I felt like I had come a long way since my first session but still had doubts about my ability to do my job.

I would be going back three and a half months after the injury, and normal recovery is six to twelve months. When I arrived for my session, Ann took me back, and when I walked into her office, I looked at the board, and it was full of tasks. I could see it was going to be business as usual with Ann for the last session, not like the last day of school where you sat around, talked, and were dismissed. Ann gave me my picture sheet with twelve pictures on it. I studied it and gave it back. I made my copy of the board and the tasks, and we were off and running.

The hour passed by fast as it usually did, and it was over! Ann and I talked about everything, from the first session till this last one.

I asked her, "How did I do in my therapy? Am I average, above average, below average? How do I stack up against the people you have worked with over your career who have had this type of injury as far as recovery and ability?"

Ann looked at me and smiled and said, "I don't know how you measure up to the others who have had your type of injury because I have no one to compare you to." I was puzzled by her response, and then she added, "I have been doing this for a long time and have never had someone who suffered the severity of the injury you have that has been as functional as you are. So I can't compare you because there really is no one even close to you. You are way above average for the injury you suffered. I would have to say it is a miracle really. You should have some sort of major deficit, but here you are. You will do fine when you go back to work, and if you need some help, just call and set up an appointment, and I will help you out."

I wasn't ready for that response. I sat there for a second letting what she said sink in. I was shocked to hear her say that and felt blessed beyond belief at God's mercy he was showing me. As we wrapped things up, I asked Ann, "Can I could give you a hug?"

She said, "Sure."

I wanted to squeeze her much harder than I did, but she is so tiny I didn't want to hurt her. I thanked her for everything and headed home. I didn't have physical therapy anymore. Josh had released me the last session, with the same offer as Ann that if I needed help, to get with him, and he would set a session up. He felt I was on the right path and was doing a good job at home.

On the drive home, I kept thinking about what Ann had said to me and the overall experience this whole thing had been for me up to this point. When I got home, and Meg got home from work, I told her what Ann had said about my progress and where I was in relation to everyone else she had worked with in relation to the injury I had. I think when I told her, she was surprised too at Ann's comment about me.

I think Meg, like me, realized there was nothing common about my whole situation right from the start.

CHAPTER 29

As December rolled on, I had been chipping away at my shopping list and was in good shape for the holiday. I just needed small stuff for everyone's stockings, and that was it.

Today, I had my consultation with Dr. Gewirtz about my surgery. We had wanted to get it done by the end of the year, but Dr. Gewirtz was booked until the second week of January. The scheduler had thrown out two dates at me. One was the twenty-first, and the other was the twenty-fourth. I picked the twenty-fourth. That was my grandmother's birthday. I figured this started on my mother's birthday, and I couldn't think of a better date to put an end to it than her birthday.

I arrived at the office, got checked in, and was taken back right after sitting down. They weighed me fully clothed with my coat on. I tipped the scales at 218 pounds. They put me in a room and said the doctor would be in shortly. I was nervous, and my hands were sweating thinking about the operation that was coming up. What really got me was how everyone, even Dr. Gewirtz, had all said I should have fallen over dead when the rupture happened, and I hadn't. My recovery had been amazing so far to the point I drove myself to this appointment. I was feeling good, getting stronger, and appreciated everything in my life, and now had to risk it all to put an end to the ticking time bomb in my head, with no guarantee I would make it through my surgery.

Dr. Gewirtz came in, and we exchanged our greetings. He started out with how the entire surgery would go. He said I would get to the hospital at 6:00 a.m. They would take me back to get the IV hooked up. The anesthesiologist would be in to see me, and shortly after that, they would take me back for the surgery.

Once in the OR, they would put me out. He would make the crescent-moon-shaped incision, cut my skull open, then go in and put the clip on the aneurysm, remove the scope, and the team would close me up. They would move me to recovery, and once awake, they would move me to ICU to spend the night, and then I would go home the next morning.

He then said, "The surgery does present some risks. Because we are talking about an invasive procedure, you could have a seizure, a stroke, a heart attack, or even die during the procedure."

That right there is the stuff that had me nervous, but I didn't have any choice if I wanted to be able to live my life the way I wanted to.

Dr. Gewirtz told me, "There is a woman in the hospital right now whom I did the same procedure on yesterday. She spent the night in ICU and is going home today."

I said, "Yeah, it's not like it's brain surgery or anything."

We both laughed, and he said, "There is a big difference in a surgery when you place a clip on an aneurysm compared to when you do a surgery after one has already ruptured. Once they have ruptured, that creates several other issues that complicate the surgery and the recovery time. In your case, you have come through the rupture very well, which is a good indicator as to how you will do with the clip placement. I have to tell you all of the things that could go wrong because they can and sometimes do happen, but I would say, based on everything and how well you're doing in your recovery, that the chances of anything going wrong during the procedure would be less than 5 percent."

I liked the numbers he was using. I like to gamble, and those were some good odds. There was that, and I felt like I was in great hands with my doctor, and those two things put my mind at ease.

I told Dr. Gewirtz, "It wasn't hard to be brave for the first surgery because I didn't even know it was going to or did happen, but this one I'm aware of, and I know what is at stake here. My recovery is going well, and now I have to risk it all again."

Dr. Gewirtz said, "The aneurysm is small, and you could wait, but sooner or later, it will need to be fixed, or one day it will rupture, and it isn't located in the best of places to fix after a rupture. I feel certain, if we do nothing, and with it in the middle of your brain, were it to rupture, your results, should you survive it, would not be the same as this time." I agreed with him, and he added, "I'm going to say that I think that you will do fine and be fine during and after the surgery."

I thanked him, and he asked if there were any more questions, then told me to stop at the desk to get set up for blood work. Then, in Dr. Gewirtz fashion, went out the door without another word.

I stopped by the desk, and the lady there gave me a card with the information for my blood draw. I thanked her and headed for home. The meeting with the doctor made me feel better, but I still had apprehension inside of my head because, it *is* brain surgery after all!

Christmas came, and we were all together again. I could have cared less if I got anything. I had all I wanted with all of us being together and sharing the day, spending time talking, eating, and relaxing in the hot tub. My family has always made the most out of any situation, and I think it's safe to say our times together now are even more focused on that. The holiday came and went. Preslie and Kam headed back to Michigan, and New Year's was upon us. We didn't do much, just staying awake to see the ball drop was a feat in itself, especially if I have a drink or two, but I save a lot of money that way.

I was to go back to work on January 7. I would work for a couple of weeks, then go out for my surgery. I would be out for another two weeks, then would go back to work full time. The only reason I was going to be out for the two weeks was so my incision could heal due to the gateway it creates to my brain.

January 7! Back to work today. The alarm went off, and I got up and got showered, dressed, then headed to the kitchen to get a bite to eat. I had toast with honey on it and a giant cup of coffee. I finished off my breakfast and left. I wanted to get there and get things rolling. My goal for the day was to get through my email and to set up my check-off lists of my daily, weekly, monthly, quarterly, semi and annual tasks so I didn't forget to do anything for compliance reasons. I was also going to meet my new boss. While I was out, my old boss had transferred to another warehouse in his home state of Wisconsin. I was hoping my new boss was going to be as good as my old boss, Ryan, had been. I really enjoyed working for Ryan but can understand why he and his family wanted to get closer to home.

When I got to work, I was met by my team in the office. There were greetings and hugs. Meg had taken me to the warehouse a couple of weeks after we got home from Spokane, and I was feeling up to it. I got to see a lot of people I knew then. Today, I was having a problem getting started because of the amount of people who were stopping by to say hello and welcome back and that they had been praying for me and they were happy I was okay and back at work. I let them know how much I appreciated the prayers, and I too was glad to be back at work. I sat down at my desk and got started on my email. As I was working my way through the emails, there were questions from my team. The phone was ringing, and I had to answer it, visitors coming in and going. The team was working through breaks, just many distractions, and I found myself overwhelmed by all of the chaos going on. It wasn't anything that I hadn't seen before. I was just having an extremely hard time staying focused on what I was doing. I was thinking back to my sessions with Ann and all the things she had added to create distractions!

This was just like that but on steroids! When I would get interrupted by someone or some situation, once I addressed the need, I couldn't remember what I was doing. I was trying hard to work through the distractions, but I wasn't doing very well. It was becoming clear that even though I had come far, I still had far to go.

After I got done with my email, I spent much of my day getting stopped by people who were welcoming me back and telling them the story of what had happened and that I had to have another surgery in a couple of weeks. When I told everyone about the second surgery, every single one of them told me they would keep me in their prayers. I told them "please do it because it matters" and that I could tell many people were praying for me by how much calm I had in me with everything that was going on.

As the day was moving on, I finally met my new boss, and he was a good guy it seemed, and that matched up with what everyone had been telling me about him. My day went by like a blur, and when I got home, my brain felt like it did after a mad session with Ann. One of the things Ann had taught me was to make a list, which I did.

Meg had been home for about an hour before I got there, and when I got in the house, she asked, "How did it go today?"

I said, "It was great to get back and see everyone."

Then she asked, "How did it go doing your job?"

I said, "It was pretty confusing at times. I made it through my emails and made a list of things to do and put it in the back pocket of my pants." As I was telling her this, I patted my pocket and pulled out the list. I had several things on the list that needed done and had failed to do one of them! I started to laugh.

Meg asked, "What's so funny?"

I told her, "I just looked at my list of things that I needed to do and hadn't done one of them."

Meg said, "I'm sure you will get them done tomorrow at work, and I'm sure you had everyone wanting to talk to you." I agreed with her and let her know that is exactly what had happened.

Second day at work was like the first day at work: much confusion and plenty of distractions. One of my favorite cartoon characters said one time, "I say, boy, you're doing a whole lot of chopping, but you're not making many chips!" And that is exactly how I was feeling about my return to work. In short, my first week back to work had breezed by, and at the end of it, I said to Meg, "I'm going to have to really pick up my game next week."

She asked, "Why?"

I said, "Because these are my lists of things to do"—I was holding a handful of papers for her to see—"and I failed to complete one task I had written down." Apparently, you can make all of the list you want, but if you never look at them, nothing will get done, so the week wasn't a total failure. I had learned something!

Meg said, "Why don't you go upstairs and work in your office up there where you can have some quiet?"

I said, "I need to be able to function in the environment in the downstairs office to be able to do my job, so I'm going to stay down there. Who knows, maybe I won't be able to do this anymore."

Meg said, "You'll be fine. Give it some time."

My thoughts were much the same as they were after my first session with Ann, *I'm just going to have to focus, and I'm going to do better next week.* I didn't think the first week was a failure; it just wasn't what I wanted it to be. My counterpart who worked weekdays, Colton, had been in the department when I got there. During the time I was out, three months, he had to do everything that needed to be done by himself—which is a lot! I felt bad he had to carry the whole load, but he had done a great job, and there was nothing that didn't get done on time.

Colton told me after I got back that he too was going to be transferring out to another warehouse. He was going back to the one he had come from. Colton and Ryan had a lot to do with me taking the position in the department when I did. I loved working with those guys. There was teamwork, and I liked them for who they were as people.

I asked Colton, "Why are you transferring back?"

He said, "I like to be busy and challenged, and this just isn't enough for me."

I thought, *Man, not enough. Having to do everything by yourself for three and a half months isn't enough.* I would soon find out exactly what he had been through because they did away with the other manager's position in my department, and I have been doing everything by myself now for a year, and I can say I'm never bored or looking for something to do!

The second week of work, things seemed to calm down. I had talked to almost everyone, and I brought back all of my check-off lists and was knocking them out as well as my new daily ones too, but the moments of confusion continued for me.

Everything was rolling along fine, then I got a call, "Hey, we have a power equipment accident on the dock. Can someone come down?" Then, "We have a riser leaking on the north wall that needs to be looked at."

Then someone walked out the front door and sets off the EAS theft system and appeared visually to have nothing on them, and then I got a call. The FDA just hit the front door, and I was as far away from the front door of the warehouse as I could possibly be.

This is exactly what my job is like on a daily basis. Everything could be going along fine, then total chaos! Lucky for me, the only decision that ever needs to be made right away is, "How bad is the bleeding, and do I need to stop the bleeding right now?" Other than that, it was just prioritizing things and then taking care of them in order.

I had someone at the front door, and they should have had the person who set off the sensor come into the office where they were on camera. Then they could go through the process of elimination to figure out what set off the sensor. That same person is who I would have had to call the company who fixes our leaks. If it was a bad leak, the rover would need to go and shut down the riser valve to stop the flow of water and have them go to the accident on the dock to document it. The FDA would be my first priority. However, my brain was trying to process everything in the order it came to me, and I was having a hard time figuring out what I needed to do first. My confusion over basic simple stuff was concerning to me.

I headed to the office and, on the way, figured out the FDA was my number one. The guy who set off the theft sensor was sitting on a chair in the office on camera as I thought he would be. My person was all over that situation. My rover let me know the leak was a small leak, and we could just monitor it and wait for the repair company to come and take care of it. So I had him go to the dock and take care of the accident at that time. The guy who set off the sensor had purchased a new pair of boots, and they had a sensor built into them, so we deactivated it so he wouldn't set it off every time he went in or out of the building. The FDA was there looking for a sample of toothpaste, which we got for them, and no one was hurt in the accident, so that was good. I had the company that takes care of our fire suppression system issues come in to fix the leak. We had a fitting that had rusted through, and they replaced it, so everything was good at that point.

My disappointment came from the fact that this should have been a breeze to figure out, but it took me several minutes to work my way through it. I could only see the confusion and lack of response when I should have been happy that I worked my way through it. I am lucky to have a very tenured group of associates on my team who handled everything as it should have been, so I'm blessed to have them on my side.

CHAPTER 30

I was outside talking to Stu one day about how work was going and my upcoming surgery. I told him I was concerned about the possible outcomes that come with the risks.

Stu said that he and Betty had been praying for me and had me on their prayer list at church, and everyone would be lifting me up in prayer on the day of the surgery too. Stu said, "You're going to do just fine, and then you can get on with your life."

I said, "I hope so."

And he replied, "You'll be fine."

I liked his confidence, and as I was sitting and thinking about it later on, I just finally accepted the fact it was going to happen, and it had to happen. I have all of these people pulling for me and praying for me, and God hadn't let me down. And I felt that he wasn't going to let me down this time either. I had a calm settle in me, and it felt amazing.

The twenty-fourth arrived. Meg got me up at 4:30 a.m. Meg got up and showered first. She always gets up first and gives me a few extra minutes to lie there. Then I got up and got ready. It's funny how when I get up most mornings, I will have coffee and toast or a muffin, not much and, most mornings, just coffee. On days when you're not allowed to eat for whatever reason, on those days, I seem to be mad dog hungry, and today was no exception.

Meg and I left the house. It was about a forty-five minute drive to the northeast side of Columbus to the hospital where my surgery was going to take place. We talked on the way, and it seemed like in no time, we were there. We parked the car. It was a beautiful, cold, crisp morning, and you could tell it was going to be a sunny day once the sun came up. We made our way inside and checked in. They came and got me to take me back to prep me.

They told Meg, "When we get him ready, we will come and get you so you can go back."

They got me a gown and some of those fancy no-slip slippers to slide on. Next, they got my IV going and hooked me up to the heart and blood pressure monitors. The anesthesiologist came in and talked me through everything and said he would see me in the OR. Meg was finally able to come back, and we were, as she would say, "Chitchatting."

She asked, "Are you scared?"

I told her, "Actually, I'm not. I feel really calm."

I have had several surgeries over my life, and this was the second biggest one I was about to have. And I was the calmest I have ever been for any surgery.

Dr. Gewirtz came in to see me. He looked at my chart and asked me, "How are you doing?"

I told him, "I'm well and ready to get this over and done." Then I asked him something that had been on my mind. I asked, "Is there a chance you could take a picture of my brain when you are doing the surgery?"

He smiled with a little laugh and said, "I don't think you would want my or your phone out in the operating room with your brain exposed."

I said, "I just thought I would ask and thought it would be a novel thing to have."

Then he said, "I do video all of my surgeries and may be able to get a still shot of it from the video, but you may have to remind me."

I was surprised and said I would remind him on one of my follow-up visits.

He said, "You do that. Do you have any other questions?"

I said, "No."

And he said, "Okay, then I'll see you in there in a little bit."

I said, "Okay." And out the door he went.

175

Meg gave me the motherly look of disgust and said, "Are you serious?"

To which, I said, "How many people have an actual photo of their own brain?" I figured, as long as it was going to happen, what the heck? I was also pretty sure that I wasn't going to get another chance for one in my lifetime, or at least hoped not!

Finally, the nurses came and got me to take me back. Meg gave me a kiss and said, "Good luck. I love you."

I said, "I'll see you in a little bit. I love you too."

And they wheeled me out. The trip to the OR didn't take long, and when we got there and they opened the door, I could tell right away it wasn't like the other operations I had. Normally, there are five or six people there. When we came through the door, there were, at my best guess, a dozen people in there, and they were all busy doing something. They got me transferred to the operating table.

One of the guys there asked me, "How are you doing?"

I said, "I'm good. How are you?"

He said, "I'm good too. Are you nervous?"

I said, "No, actually this is the calmest I have ever been for a surgery."

He looked at me with a surprised look on his face and said, "Well, that's good."

I said, "I'm ready to get this surgery over with so I can get on with my life. I have total confidence in Dr. Gewirtz, and you all are professionals here and know what you're doing, so I trust you all and know I'm in good hands."

He said, "That's great, and you are in good hands!"

The anesthesiologist came in and told me he was going to take good care of me during the operation and asked if I had any questions before he put me under, which I didn't.

As he was pushing the syringe in my IV, I heard him say, "Gonna feel a little cold."

I always see how long I can hang on before lights out and try counting to see how far I can get. Two is the number I recall getting to before going out this time. If you have never been put under, it is like fading into nothingness. You don't dream, or if you do, I don't remember them. It is like a big void in time.

Then I recall hearing, "Kelley, can you wiggle your fingers and toes for us?" Then I heard it again. Can I wiggle my fingers and toes? I thought, *Why is someone asking me that?* Then I remembered, *Oh yeah, the surgery!* I wiggled my fingers and toes. I then thought that's a good thing that I could do that and understand what they were saying to me. Then I was asked, "Kelley, can you open your eyes?"

I opened my eyes and was met with a couple of smiling faces. At that moment, my thoughts were, *No way. I'm going to get out of this again with nothing wrong with me!* The nurses asked me my questions, the same ones I messed up for a month in Spokane, and I got them all right the first try. Unbelievable! What a moment! I looked at the clock on the wall, and it was 10:45 a.m. The whole process didn't take three hours!

The nurses were talking to me and were telling me they would get me to the ICU as soon as I had something to eat and drink. I laid there a bit groggy, with my eyes shut. I wished Nana a happy birthday and thanked her for being with me. I felt her presence with me and knew it had something to do with how calm I was, that and all of the prayers that had been going out for me.

The nurse came in and asked, "Would you like a drink of water?"

I said, "Yeah, that sounds good."

Then she asked, "Do you think you can eat something?"

I said, "I'll give it a try."

I was thinking about my incision being on my right temple and wasn't sure how it would feel, but I was about to find out. The nurse brought me water and crackers. I hit the water pretty hard and she asked, "Do you want to try a cracker?"

I said, "Sure."

She gave me one, and I got it down with no trouble and kept it down. I had another cracker and finished my water. A short time later, they moved me to the ICU.

Once I was in the ICU, It wasn't long until Meg came in. She asked, "How are you feeling?"

I told her, "I feel good considering a guy was just in the middle of my brain." Meg laughed. "Can you believe I'm going to get out of this again and won't have to worry about it anymore?"

Meg replied, "Yep, you're good to go. Dr. Gewirtz said everything went great. He said he was only in the OR for forty-five minutes, placed the clip, and they closed you up after he left."

What a true blessing people like Dr. Gewirtz, and Dr. Carlson are to us all, to be able to do what they do and not give it a second thought. When I was a kid, if someone was having brain surgery, there was a very good chance they weren't going to fare very well after the surgery, if they even survived it. Now it's you go into the hospital, have the surgery, spend the night, and go home the next day fine!

Meg asked, "Does your head hurt?"

I said, "All things considered, not much at all. I was a little concerned when I ate the cracker, based on how a person's temple moves, if it would hurt or not, but it was okay."

Meg stuck around for most of the day, then went home. I slept most of the day and watched some TV, had my dinner which was soup, pudding, crackers, and Jell-O. There's always room for Jell-O, right?

My sleep that night was interrupted throughout the night by the nursing staff coming in and checking on me. I wasn't really all that tired anyhow since I had been sleeping most of the day. The night passed and gave way to the morning.

I woke up, and they brought me breakfast. As I was eating, I could see Dr. Gewirtz making his rounds with a few people in tow. They made their way to my room and came in.

We said our hellos, and the doctor asked me, "How are you feeling?"

I said, "I'm fine. I don't have much pain. My mind is fine, my motor skills are fine, and I'm just waiting to go home."

Dr. Gewirtz said, "That's great! They are going to come and get you out of bed and put you through some exercises to see how you do with them. If you do well, they will get things wrapped up, and you will be discharged after that."

I said, "That sounds good to me." Dr. Gewirtz started to walk out of the room, and I called, "Dr. Gewirtz!" He stopped and turned around and looked at me. "I want you to know you're a true blessing from God, and I can never thank you enough for what you have done for me and my family."

He smiled and said, "Maybe you can take me on an elk hunt someday." Then out the door he went.

I thought about it and thought, *That would be an excellent idea*, and something I would certainly consider doing.

Not long after he had left, the physical therapy team showed up and asked if I was ready to get out of bed and do some work. I was. They had me sit upon the side of my bed and see if I felt dizzy at all, and I didn't. Then I stood up at the side of the bed, and I was fine with that. They put a fall restraint belt on me and asked me how I felt. I told them I felt fine and was ready to go. We started off just walking the hallways for a bit. Then we walked with me placing one foot per square on the floor tile for some time to check my balance out even more. No problems with that. We moved to the staircase next. We went down a couple of floors first. They asked how I was feeling. I told them I was fine, and we could head back up. I did get a bit winded when we reached the top, and we stopped till I caught my breath, then headed back down. We did this a few times.

When we reached the top the third time, the therapist said, "Good job. I think you're good to be discharged. I will get the paperwork going when we get back."

I said, "Good deal. I feel ready to go."

We headed back to the ICU, and when we got there, Meg was waiting on us. She asked how I did.

The therapist said, "He did good, and I think he is ready to go home. I'm going to get the paperwork going, and we will get you two on your way as soon as possible."

Meg said, "Sounds good," then she asked me, "How do you feel?"

I said, "I feel good. My head doesn't hurt much at all, and I slept pretty good considering how many times they woke me up to check on me. And I am ready to go home." Then she asked if Dr. Gewirtz had been in. I told her what I said to him and his response about going elk hunting.

She said, "Would you really take him?"

I said, "Sure, I would, if he really wanted to go."

She smiled and shook her head a little bit. I guess she couldn't understand the thought of me going back to Montana and up into the mountains after what had happened. I used to say that my perfect death would be if I went elk hunting, and I didn't return. Then when they sent out a search team, they found me dead of a heart attack with my recurve bow in my hand and a big bull elk lying dead a short way off with my arrow in his heart! I repeated that scenario so many times in my life to people, and now after what happened to me, I can say I am wrong! I don't want that to be how I go. The mountains are beautiful, but they are also a lonely place. After my experience, I have decided my perfect death is to die an old man lying in my bed at home surrounded by those I love and the ones who love me the most, not away from them on a lonely mountain top! There was nothing I wanted more when my aneurysm ruptured than Meg and the girls, just to be able to tell them I love them. I was so sure that wasn't going to happen and knew there was only one way it could, and that was God! I had mentioned earlier that I was wheeling and dealing with God to let me see them again, and I would do anything he wanted me to. Well, here I am writing this for you to read.

I said before that my daughter Payten is my bike riding buddy and has been since she was seven. One day after my second surgery, when I had healed up and spring had sprung, we went for our first bike ride in a long time. Columbus has a great bike system of paved biking trails around and through it. She and I have logged over a thousand miles on those trails since moving into the area. We do between twenty to thirty miles a trip.

On this ride, we were cruising along, and I said, "How lucky are we that we still get to do this?"

She said, "Yeah, I know."

We rode out ten miles, and there is a park with some restrooms there. Payten said she needed to use the restroom. There was a woman sitting there reading the Bible. Payten went into the restroom, and I took off my helmet and my sweat band.

I said to the woman, "I see you're reading the Good Book."

She said, "I'm reading the truth."

I said, "Ain't that the truth!"

We both laughed a little, and she said, "What happened to you?" pointing at my head.

I said, "Oh, I had a brain aneurysm rupture on the artery to my brain while I was in the mountains of Montana elk hunting," and added, "I'm writing a book about the whole thing but haven't worked on it much lately because when it's nice out, we are always busy going places and doing things, so I don't have as much time as I do in the wintertime."

Now I see a lot of people looking at my head because it is unique, but if they see me looking at them looking at me, they always look away. Not one person has ever asked me about what happened. Payten and I have ridden this trail plenty of times, and I have never seen this woman before or since that day who, to me, seemed to have a Jamaican accent.

The woman looked right at me and said, "You need to finish your book. God wants you to brag about him!"

At that moment, I never for one second thought that what she said was her opinion on the situation. I have always believed from that very moment that was a direct message from God!

That is a moment I think about a lot because a couple of days later, I was reading my Bible. Our church gives us journals every year at the beginning of the year that have daily verses to read. I had been reading in Psalms, and Psalms 50:15 reads, "And call upon me in the day of trouble: I will deliver thee, and thou shalt glorify me." I read that over and over. There was the *truth* staring me right in the face, the deal I made with God walking out of the mountains the day it happened. He had more than held up his end of the deal, and I had so many people telling me you need to write a book about it. It is a great story. The message from the woman and now the message from God are right in my face.

I made a full commitment to finish the book as soon as possible. I could say that everything that had happened since the rupture was a coincidence, but wow, what an unbelievable amount of coincidences to happen in this case.

Payten came out of the restroom. I bid the woman a good day. She said, "The same to you," with a smile on her face.

That encounter to me, along with the Bible verse two days later, just reinforced God is real, even if you don't add in the fact three great doctors all said I should have fallen over dead, and that there was nothing wrong with me. There are so many reasons I should be dead, but I'm not, and I am fine. As the doctor in Missoula said, "I don't like to use the word miracle, but in your case, I don't know what else to say. You should have fallen over dead."

Meantime, back at the hospital, the nurse came back with a list of dos and don'ts, a prescription for pain meds, and some wound instructions. She told us what to look for, and if X, Y, or Z happened, we needed to come to the hospital ASAP. Then I was discharged. They gave me a ride to the front door in a wheelchair even though I told them I could walk it. Once we were at the entrance, I got out of the wheelchair, and Meg and I walked out the front door to the car. It was another bright sunny day, cold and crisp just like the day before when we arrived there. I was full of joy and peace knowing I didn't have to worry about aneurysms anymore. My head felt pretty good, and the ride went by fast.

CHAPTER 31

We pulled up into the driveway. It was about two in the afternoon. Everything went just as Dr. Gewirtz had said it would, thirty-eight hours from the time we left until we returned home, with a trip to the middle of my brain in between. The afternoon was filled with phone calls from family and friends wanting to know how I was and how the surgery had gone. I have to say the amount of love and concern poured out for me by so many was amazing. I spent the day on the phone, napping, and watching TV. I was thinking, *Now that I don't have to worry about a ticking time bomb in my head, as soon as Dr. Gewirtz releases me, I'm going to get in the best shape I can because I have a plan!*

Meg cooked dinner for us, and I was actually pretty hungry. I was thinking that eating would be painful because I had been on a soft diet at the hospital and due to the location of the incision and how your temple moves when you chew. Surprisingly, I had little to no pain when I chewed, so I went at my dinner like a ravenous animal. We finished dinner and spent the evening watching TV. Then we went to bed.

When we left the hospital and got in the car, I pulled down the visor and flipped up the mirror cover to have a look at my new feature on my head. I remember Dr. Gewirtz had said "I'll make a three- to four-inch incision right here in a crescent moon shape" while moving his index finger in a curving motion over my temple area. When I looked in the mirror, I remember thinking, *That's three or four inches?* The incision had fifteen staples holding it shut. It went from the outside end of my right eyebrow in a crescent shape over my temple and down past my right ear to the bottom of my ear. Definitely not three or four inches, but I really didn't care. I had a little bruising around my eye and a small spot of blood in the outside white part of my eye.

The next morning when I woke up, I had a new look. My eye was in full bloom, dark purple under the eye with a rainbow of color the rest of the way around it, and the white parts of my eye were full bloody. My ear area was still yellow from stuff they used to sterilize the area. I looked a bit "demonic," I said when I would send someone that picture. My head didn't hurt much at the new incision site, but the original site still hurt all of the time, but it was getting better little by little.

That day went by pretty uneventfully, and even though I looked rough, I felt pretty good. That night, I was pretty tired and went to bed early. During the night, I woke up with a bad headache. I got out of bed and went to the kitchen and took a pain pill and went back to bed. When I woke up the next time, not only was my head still going full bore, I was feeling like I needed to throw up! Meg was up and out of bed as I was lying there. I was trying to figure out what had changed since I had gone to bed to make me feel this bad.

As I was lying there, I was pretty sure that I was going to throw up, so I got out of bed and went into the bathroom. It was strange that I was fine for two days, and now I was feeling this bad. I thought maybe I had spent a lot of time sleeping on my incision during the night, and that's what had my head hurting so bad. Then there was the feeling like I was going to throw up, which I really didn't want to happen with my head feeling the way it did. I hadn't given it much thought till then, but we did eat pretty early, and I most likely had taken the pain meds on an empty stomach, which may have something to do with how I was feeling now. Either way, it was a bad morning for me and was about to get worse.

I was in the bathroom, and I could tell the moment I was hoping wouldn't come came. I thought I was going to throw up, but the tank must have been empty, and I ended up having the dry heaves. Good Lord, what misery! I was hoping I didn't pop any staples out of my head as I was straining so hard during the whole thing. I had a few rounds of the heaves and started to feel like the feeling was subsiding but decided to stay put, just in case it was a false reading on what was really going on. After a half an hour had gone by with no more episodes, I decided to go out to the living room.

Meg asked, "Are you okay?"

I said, "I don't know what's up, if I slept on my incision, and that gave me a headache or what, but I took a pill, and I didn't think about it being so long since I had anything to eat. But I had the dry heaves, and it really sucked."

Meg said, "Oh, hon, do you want to try to eat or drink something now?"

That was a no for me. I was worried that if I ate or drank anything at this point, I would have another bout and didn't want that. My head hurt the way it did when my first aneurysm had ruptured, so much so it was worse when I had my eyes open, so I sat on the love seat with my eyes closed and my head propped up, with my elbow on the arm of the love seat. Meg called the hospital and told them my situation. They thought that me taking the pill on an empty stomach was probably the reason for my nausea and said I should eat something, and if my head got worse, that we may want to think about coming in to get it looked at. I sure didn't want to go for a car ride, but I would if I had too.

I felt sick all day, and I just couldn't bring myself to eat anything for fear of throwing up or heaving again. I went to bed pretty much feeling the way I did when I woke up. The next morning, I woke up to the same situation. I still felt nauseous, and the headache was still raging on. I was extremely hungry and couldn't stand it anymore, so I decided to eat some honey toast and hoped it would stay down. I got the toaster out, put the bread in, and hit the plunger down. I got a cup of milk while the bread was toasting. It smelled great. When it popped up, I gave it the butter and honey treatment and wasted no time in eating it. Even though it was just toast, it tasted amazing, and it was gone in short order. I went to the living room and turned on the TV.

Meg got up and came out of the bedroom and asked me, "How are you feeling?"

I said, "My headache is still raging, and my stomach is still upset, but I was so hungry I ate some honey toast, and I'm waiting to see what happens."

Meg said, "Well, if you don't feel better later on, let's go to the hospital and have them check you over."

I reluctantly said, "Okay."

As I was watching TV, my gut was rumbling and rolling, but it had been empty for thirty hours, and I wasn't feeling any worse, so for me, it was a so-far-so-good, thing. As the morning wore on, I actually felt a little better, and at lunch, I decided to eat again. I had some chicken noodle soup and crackers, then went back to the couch, and as the day went by, my headache returned to the normal level, and my stomach calmed down. I ate dinner and felt pretty normal again. It must have been the pill on an empty stomach that had me all jacked up, but it was over now. The next day, I woke up feeling good and got back on my exercise routine because I had a plan.

My plan was something I had promised my good friend Dan, whom I met when he was about ten years old. Dan's mom watched our girls when they were little while we were at work. Dan's family had welcomed our family into their family holiday celebrations like we were their own. We would all meet at the "Barn" to have holiday meals and share time and conversations.

I started hunting with Dan when he was in high school. I would take him turkey hunting on his family's farm. He has done well since starting. To the best we can figure, he is seventeen for seventeen at this point. Anyhow, I had promised Dan I would take him elk hunting someday, and that is just what I aimed to do that fall. I needed to get back in mountain shape with the time I had left until the season opened. I was following my restrictions Dr. Gewirtz had given me as well as following the restrictions Dr. Megan had given me.

There is nothing but truth in the saying, "Happy wife, happy life!" I didn't have any more episodes of nausea or my head hurting more than usual after that one time, and I never took any more pain pills without food either.

The day came for me to go back to Dr. Gewirtz to get my staples out. I drove myself there, got checked in, and was taken back before I could even sit down. I got weighed, and they put me in a room, was asked the usual questions, and said he would be in shortly.

Dr. Gewirtz came in, and we talked about how the recovery was going. I told him about the episode I had. He thought that maybe I had slept on my incision for an extended period of time, and me taking the pain med on an empty stomach is most likely what had made me nauseous. Dr. Gewirtz said the incision area looked great and proceeded to take the staples out. While he was taking them out, he confirmed the incision was secure, so one less thing to worry about.

He asked, "When are you going back to work?"

I said, "In three days."

He asked me, "How did it go when you went back the first time?"

I said, "I struggled with confusion when things get hectic but was using the skills Ann had taught me to help me through those times. I also get fatigued after a couple of days of work, but I work two days, then have two off, then work two days and have one off, so it gives my brain time to rest."

He said, "That's great. I'm going to set you up for one more visit, and as long as everything is good, I will release you after that visit."

I said, "That sounds great to me. What about my limits?"

He said, "You can do whatever you want at this point. If you feel like you're doing too much, back it down a little, but you can do whatever you want."

I thanked him again for everything and went to see the scheduler to set up my last appointment, then headed home.

I told Meg when she got home that I only had one more visit in a month, and as long as everything was going good, he was going to release me. She was happy to hear that almost as much as I was.

I had been in contact with Dan and let him know it was time to apply for our elk tags. We each applied on our own, which in the past was how Dirsch and I had done it and had always both drawn tags. This time, for whatever reason, Dan didn't get drawn, but I did. Dan called me and said that even though he wasn't drawn, he still wanted to go and would get the upland game bird and fishing licenses and apply for anything else he could in the special draws. I was so happy he still wanted to go and excited to have his company along on the trip.

I told Dan we need to get in shape—well, Dan is in great shape. He is a lineman for the utilities and gets plenty of exercise, that and he's half my age. So I should have said, "I need to get in shape." I know after the events from last year's hunt, Meg was glad Dan still wanted to go with me, to say the least.

CHAPTER 32

The spring of that year, we went to Florida for a week's vacation. Meg is our travel agent, and she does a great job of finding us a nice place to stay, car, and all flight arrangements. She spends a lot of hours looking and planning on the computer to ensure that we are comfortable and have a great time. She has done this so many times, I think other than picking the place to stay, the rest of it is a breeze for her. On this trip, there would be me, Meg, Preslie, Payten, Kam, and Payten's friend Emily. Preslie and Kam would be flying from Ft. Wayne and the rest of us from Columbus. Our flights would be arriving within an hour of each other. We would get the rental car and then drive to Anna Maria Island from Tampa, about an hour drive.

When we arrived at the rental and went inside, it was great, very clean, comfortable, and private. There was a small pool in the back, and the place was fenced all the way around. I can say we were all happy with Meg's work on this project. For me, the place was perfect. Not only was it nice, it was within walking distance to several great hangouts and places to eat, but the best part was getting to spend time with everyone. It was on this trip that I actually started on this book. What I mean by that is up until now, I said I was working on a book but, in fact, had only been logging notes and dates of events down. I thought I was writing a book, but I wasn't telling a story; I was just logging data which has proven to be very helpful. But on this trip, I actually started to write the story. I would get up early and work on the book for a couple of hours, and then around noon, Meg and I would go for a walk on the beach.

The beach was a couple of blocks away, but we didn't mind the walk to it. Daily, there are problems to solve, and for Meg and I, daily it was "Which way do you want to walk today?" For anyone who has never seen the ocean, make time and go. It will amaze you and humble you as to just how small you really are, and if you want to be humbled even more, get in it. If you do go to the beach, make sure to make time to take in a sunrise or a sunset. Both are things of beauty. One cool thing about walking the beach is you can walk the same stretch of beach daily, and it will be different every day! The water level depends on where the tide is in its cycle. The things you see washed up on the beach overnight are different every day—seashells, dead sea creatures, jellyfish, octopus, crabs, fish. Then there are the things you see in the water like dolphins, boats, parasailers, surfers, cruise ships, and even though you may see some of the same things, every trip is never the same. I think that the walks on the beach are good for the soul. I can't tell you exactly what it is, but when you walk the beach, you know it is something special and a gift to enjoy.

We would either go to the beach for the day or hang out at the pool. This year, we were lucky. We happened to hit the love bug hatch perfectly. For those who have never seen it, they are everywhere! So we partied with the love bugs and the lizards too. Florida has these little lizards that are everywhere. I think they look cool and are fun to watch. It's too bad they don't eat love bugs!

When the girls were little, we had a pool at the house, and they and their friends were in that thing all summer long. The girls were in the pool and were playing a game they used to play when they were kids, and as I was watching them play that game as young adults, I was able to see them as young girls for a brief moment playing that game and thought to myself how blessed I was to be able to be sitting there watching them and enjoying that moment.

Dinners were a mix of going out to eat or cooking at the house. It didn't matter to me what we did or where we went, so I left that up to the ladies. Whatever they decided was fine with me. I was just the chauffeur. I did let Kam take over as chauffeur a time or two on this trip. I must say he did a great job, and I have considered delegating that task to him on a permanent basis going forward. You can miss a lot when you're the driver all the time.

Before we came to Florida I was talking to a guy I work with, Michael, who has been to Anna Maria Island a lot, and he hooked me up with several good places to eat and gave me the name of a guy to go fishing with, Captain Ryan. Mike also gave me Captain Ryan's phone number, and I had called him to set up a date for Kam and me to go fishing with him. I try to go fishing when I go to Florida every time. There are fish in the ocean that are on my bucket list to catch.

Kam and I set out early on the morning of the fishing trip. We were going to meet up with Captain Ryan at 6:00 a.m. to go with him while he caught the bait fish for our trip. We had nothing better to do, and I was interested to see him in action. We got to the dock and met up with him at his slip. We introduced ourselves, loaded up what we had brought, and we headed across the bay to an area where the old bridge went across the bay from the mainland to the island. The sun hadn't broken the horizon, but it was light enough to see, and the birds were in flight.

On the way over to the bridge area, Captain Ryan had taken a bag that looked like a dog food bag and dumped some of the chum in a bucket and put some water in the bucket, turning it into a paste. When we got to the bridge, he positioned the boat and put his trolling motor in the water, and it was on auto, so it held the position while he got ready to get the bait fish. He got the bucket and the casting net. He began gathering the net up to be able to cast it out. He put the rope in his mouth and began the process of putting the weights into his hand. He paused for a moment and put some chum in the water, and it began to settle down into the darkness of the water, then he continued to gather up the net. It probably took him a full minute to get the net ready. Then he threw the net out and let it settle down into the dark water where he had put the chum. Then he started to draw the net up, and when he got it all the way up to the surface, it looked like there were a hundred fish in the net. He took the net over to the live well and dumped them in. Some of the fish fell to the floor of the boat. He picked a couple of them up and put

191

them in the well, then went back to gathering up the net again after he put some more chum in the water.

About that time, we were in the middle of a hostile takeover of the boat by several snowy egrets. They were descending upon us from all angles, and they were fearless of us. Kam and I were enjoying just watching the birds. They are about two and a half feet tall, white feathers, black legs, yellow feet, long black bill, with a small yellow patch of skin at the base of their bill. They are cool looking, to say the least. Something else they are is opportunistic! They landed on the boat and snatched up all of the fish that had fallen on the deck—in seconds. As the birds picked up the fish and swallowed them, you could see them slide down inside their long necks. Each time Captain Ryan pulled up the net, the birds were loving it as they snatched up all the ones who missed the live wells. In between the times he pulled the nets up, the birds simply walked along the sides of the boat to the live wells and just started to eat them right out of the live wells. It was a fish buffet for the birds, all you could eat.

We weren't the only ones after bait fish; there were a couple of other boats around. Captain Ryan said the one guy sold the bait-fish to local bait shops. There were also a couple of dolphins around that were taking advantage of the situation too. When any fish fell overboard, they snagged them up in short order as the sun had just broken over the horizon. Captain Ryan kept throwing the net, and we figured that he was stocking up for the next few days on bait.

We asked him if that is what he was doing, and he said, "No, we will use all of them today!"

Kam and I looked at each other and said, "Man, we must be going to catch a ton of fish today." If we were going to use all of the bait fish, we were in for a treat today because he had to have pulled several hundred on board by now. The live wells were so full the bait fish were jumping out of them and back into the water or falling on the deck, and the cleanup crew was eating them within seconds after they hit. By now, some of the birds were getting pretty full, and what goes in must come out. The birds were crapping all over the sides and deck of the boat.

Captain Ryan, satisfied with his haul, started to idle out of the area. Once clear of all of the old pylons, he throttled up and headed toward the new bridge that spans the gap between the mainland and the island. Captain Ryan asked Kam to drive the boat while he rigged up some rods for us. Kam gladly took the helm with a smile on his face and kept the course for the bridge. The drive over to where Captain Ryan wanted to go took several minutes. Once we arrived there, he took over control of the boat. The flock of egrets and some seagulls had followed the floating buffet out to the bridge and were making quite a racket. Captain Ryan pulled the boat up under the bridge and lowered his trolling motor into the water and set it on auto so it would hold the boat in that position while we fished. The wind was blowing in from open water to under the bridge, and that was producing some good-size waves. I was surprised that the trolling motor held the boat in position with them coming as fast as they were and as big as they were.

Captain Ryan got a couple of rods, hooked up some of our fresh bait fish and told us, "Cast toward the pylons with the bail open and watch your line. When it takes off, close your bail and lift your rod."

Roger that, and we both let them fly. Kam hooked up first with a grouper. It looked like it was putting up a good fight, and when he got the fish to the boat, it was about eight pounds. We were off and running. Not long after that, I hooked a grouper of my own, and shortly after that, Kam had his second one on. Capt. Ryan was moving back and forth between the two of us, removing the fish and replacing our bait on our hooks. He had no trouble keeping up with the two of us no matter how fast we were catching fish.

Captain Ryan had just taken a grouper off of my hook, tossed it back in, and put on another bait fish. I cast it right along the pylon, and as soon as the bait hit the water, it took right off. I closed the bail and lifted up, felt the pull, and set the hook. I was hooked up, and I knew whatever it was, it was big.

I yelled out, "I'm hooked up to something big."

Captain Ryan came over and said, "Tarpon!"

I was pumped because tarpon is one of my bucket list fish. I was wondering how he knew since we hadn't seen the fish.

I asked, "How do you know it's a tarpon?"

He said, "I saw your line take off as soon as your bait hit the water, and the fish headed for open water out from under the bridge as soon as you hooked him, classic tarpon behavior."

I figured he knows, so I was not going to question his assessment of the situation. Besides, the fish did head for the open water as soon as I hooked into him, and Captain Ryan had taken up chase after the fish with the boat.

I had my rod tucked up under my arm and was leaning back with all of my weight on him. The fish was swimming out in front of the boat at a steady pace and was pulling line off the reel at a slow and steady pace, even with us following him. Kam had put down his rod and was recording the event from the back of the boat. I had been getting in better shape for my return to Montana, but I can tell you just hanging onto that rod and knowing how long it can take to get a tarpon in, I was having some serious doubts about my endurance and strength to get it done by myself but was up for the challenge.

Kam had moved around the wheelhouse and was now behind me. In the video, you could see me leaning back, the rod bent, and Kam said to me, "Hey, Holmes."

I turned my head and looked over my shoulder at him with the biggest smile on my face, and "Snap!" My line broke. My rod sprung back straight, and my smile was gone.

Captain Ryan said, "I would say over hundred pounder for sure based on the way he acted and pulled."

It wasn't a catch, but what a great experience to be able to feel that kind of power generated by a fish for several minutes. I was disappointed but excited at the same time.

Captain Ryan turned the boat around and headed right back under the bridge. Once there, we both cast out again. We both caught a few more grouper, and then Kam hooked into a monster fish. I was thinking that he had hooked a tarpon too, but the fight was much different. I worked my way around the boat. I saw Kam up against the side of the boat, his rod tucked up under his arm and down over the side almost straight down, banging against the boat violently!

Kam looked at me with his eyebrows raised, eyes wide open, and an "Oh crap" look on his face. I cracked up!

Captain Ryan called, "Goliath grouper."

Kam is a strong guy, and he was in the fight, which was a whirlwind of a battle. The fish was pulling Kam into the side of the boat while slamming the rod into the boat over and over again. I was watching with great anticipation wondering what the outcome would be. I didn't have to wait long. "Snap," the line broke! I felt bad his line broke because I'm sure the look on his face mirrored the look I had on my own face not too long ago.

I said, "That was awesome. How did it feel? Was that thing pulling as hard as it looked like he was?"

Kam said, "Yeah, man. He almost took my rod from me!"

We were both laughing at the encounter and how violent it had been. We hadn't been fishing long, but if the rest of the day continued on like this, it was going to be one to talk about forever.

We fished a little longer, and Captain Ryan said, "Reel them in, guys. We're going to try another spot."

We both reeled in, and Captain Ryan had us underway. Kam and I both sat on a giant cooler that was on the deck, in front of the wheelhouse. It was the size of a chest freezer. We talked about the start of the trip and were cracking up at everything that had happened so far, especially the looks we got to see on each other's faces. To say we were having a good time was an understatement!

After a short ride across the bay, we came around a bend and pulled up on a spot where you could see the water had very clear changes in color due to changes where it dropped off into deeper water. The water was much calmer. With all of the turns we had made, the land made some nice windbreaks for us, but without the breeze, it felt fifteen degrees hotter.

Captain Ryan told us to get our rods. He picked up one of those plastic big-barreled kids bats that had the end cut off it was cut in a curving taper a little way down the barrel of the bat.

Captain Ryan said, "Cast your bait into the middle of where the fish land."

Then he went over to the live well and put about three scoops of fish in the bat with a small net that was in the live well. While he was standing behind us, he let her rip. I could hear the fish flying past my head and ducked.

Captain Ryan said, "You don't need to duck. I won't hit you."

I thought, *Yeah, right. You won't until you do.*

The fish hit the water. We both cast out into where they had landed. Our bait hit the water as the rings were dispersing from the chum hitting the water, and boom, boom, just that fast, we were both hooked up with snook! This was the first time either of us had caught a snook. I can say snook are solid fighters! We were hooking into one every cast. Our fun meters were buried in the red once again. We fished that drop off for quite a ways and caught some nice fish and caught a lot of fish.

The temps kept climbing, and on a boat in the direct sunlight in the heat of the day, it can get downright Tarzan hot!

We were both wearing UV-ray-blocking shirts, face/neck gaiters, and my hat had an extra-long bill and a neck flap that is also made of UV-blocker material. We were also using liberal amounts of sunblock and drinking lots of water, but I could tell we were both still getting plenty of sun. Our snook spot started to fizzle out but never stopped completely. We were still catching fish, just not at the pace we had been so. Captain Ryan told us to reel in. We were moving again.

We moved deeper inland. The scenery was awesome, and the deeper we went, the cover turned into mangrove clusters, and I was thinking it was looking like tarpon territory in there. We rolled up on a spot that was like a big intersection with lots of room to cast in different directions. Captain Ryan loaded up the bat and let it fly. We both cast into the impact area, and both were instantly hooked up again. Kam landed the biggest snook either of us had caught to that point. Whatever I had on was a great fight but not like any fight I had so far during the day. The fish had awesome pulling power! I fought the fish for a few minutes and finally got it in close enough that Captain Ryan got a look at it.

He said, "It's a redfish."

I was an instant fan of the redfish, great fighters and an awesome fish to look at! I have seen them caught on TV before, but that was my first one. Captain Ryan asked if he could get some pictures of the two fish because they were both pretty good size. He snapped off a few shots, and we were back at it.

Not long after that, a big fish breached about fifty yards out. All three of us saw it. It was a giant snook.

Captain Ryan told Kam, "Quick, get a cast back there."

Kam squared up to the spot and cast it out in that direction. His bait literally landed within three feet of where the big fish had come up. It was clear from what I saw the big fish was at least four feet long, maybe bigger, but at least four feet, a giant compared to all the other ones we had caught so far. It couldn't have been more than two seconds after the bait hit the water; the fish hit it, and it was on. The water erupted, and Kam's drag was at a high-pitch squeal as the line spun off his reel, with the fish headed right for the mangroves.

Captain Ryan said, "You've got to get him turned. Don't let him get in those mangroves."

Kam was doing everything he could to turn the fish. But he was having none of that. I don't know for sure if the fish made the mangroves or not. I think he did, and the line broke. Kam had done all he could, I think, but just couldn't get the fish turned. We were all talking about just how big the brute had been. It would have been nice to see it up close, but we all got a good look at him when he had jumped, and he was a class up from all of the others we had caught; that was for sure.

We also caught some jack crevalle in this spot too. I can say I am a fan of the jack crevalle too. They fight great. We caught fish all day. We had a half an hour where it was slow, but other than that, it was nonstop action from the drop of the green flag to the checkered flag. We caught fourteen different species of fish and boated over seventy fish in an eight-hour trip! To this point, this was the best Florida fishing trip I've been on hands down!

When we got back to the dock, we thanked Captain Ryan over and over. I felt he was happy with the trip too. I wasn't sure what he thought of us at first when we got into the fish. Every time either of us caught a fish, we would yell, "Look at him flop!" let's say in an old hilljack manner. One time, I looked back at Captain Ryan. He was squatting down with his back to us as Kam was yelling, "Look at him flop!" and I could see he was clearly laughing pretty hard.

We told him we had an outstanding time, and he said, "Well, if you're ever back down here and want to go fishing, give me a call."

I said, "I will for sure."

On the way back to the house, I didn't know if Kam was as tired as I was or not. We talked and laughed about everything that had happened. When we got to the house, the girls were just about ready to go out to eat. Kam and I showered and got dressed to go out.

Meg asked, "How was it?"

We told her, "It was fantastic, and if we ever come back here, we will be going with Captain Ryan again."

We went out to eat dinner at a place close to the house. We walked over to it. We had a small wait, but it didn't matter. It was beautiful out, and we had some adult beverages to enjoy as we waited. Our days were full of fun and sun, relaxation, and time spent with the ones we love. As all vacations seem to go, it was over just like that.

CHAPTER 33

We returned home, and my focus was on the trip to Montana at that point. I still had to go to, hopefully, my last appointment with Dr. Gewirtz too. On the day of that appointment, it was beautiful out, a nice cool morning with lots of sunshine. The drive up wasn't bad. It was after rush hour, and I was excited to hear those words! After arriving and being taken back to a room, I don't know why, but it seemed like forever till Dr. Gewirtz came into the room.

We had our greetings, and he asked, "How are you feeling?"

I said, "I'm feeling better daily."

Then he asked, "How is work going?"

I told him, "Work is going better than the last time we met. I'm using my skills I was taught, and they are helping me to be thorough in completing my tasks at work. The confusion continues for me during the hectic times but not to the same degree as before, and it seems to continue to improve."

Dr. Gewirtz and I didn't really spend a whole lot of time on me and my struggles because there really wasn't much given my situation and what had happened. Dr. Gewirtz told me this would be our last appointment. He was releasing me.

Then something happened that I never was expecting or even thought was possible. Dr. Gewirtz and I had a conversation about him and me. We talked about his family and mine and things we like to do in our spare time, places we like to eat around Columbus. We talked about a new rifle he had just bought and how he has it set up and his hunting experiences and some of mine, our thoughts on being parents, our kids. It was just two guys getting to know each other a little better. I would say the conversation lasted twenty minutes, and I know for me, I will always appreciate that conversation. I had a whole new way to look at Dr. Gewirtz. I knew him as a great doctor and now knew much more about Dr. Gewirtz, the man. I don't know if that conversation is something that happens between him and all of his patients, but I'm thankful it happened to me! When I think about what he does for a living and what I do for a living, and they are so, so different, but at the end of the day, we are both husbands, fathers, sons, hardworking guys who actually have much in common.

After our conversation, we shook hands, and I told him, "Let me know when you're ready to go elk hunting."

Dr. Gewirtz, if you ever read this I want you to know the offer still stands.

When I left, I was full of joy and couldn't wait to tell Meg about our conversation. When Meg got home from work, and we were eating dinner, I told her about our conversation. I think she was as surprised as I had been.

Meg said, "I'm glad you two had a chance to have that talk. He sounds like a regular guy."

I said, "Yes, he is, and he doesn't have a regular job but does have a great gift."

We agreed on that.

As the summer rolled on, I spent my time shooting my bow and getting in shape. Me and my riding buddy, Payten, were putting on the miles when she could. She had picked up a job for the summer that was eating up some of her time, but we were still going, and when she couldn't go, I was going by myself. I was finding, since my injury, I was still able to log the miles in the same amount of time, but after the rides, I was zonked!

I used to recover in half an hour, then would go and do other things. Now when I was done riding, I would take a shower and lie around or take a nap. I also noticed the heat really seemed to knock it out of me now. On days of ninety degrees or more is when I really could tell the difference. I felt it was from the injury, but it could have been the fact I was fifty-seven too. Either way, I was different now, and I was fine with it.

I have three bikes and had been talking to Dan and told him I wanted to bring one up to Michigan for him to ride. Shortly after, I was going up to see Preslie and Kam and hauled a bike up for Dan to ride. I dropped it off at his house. I said before, Dan is in great shape, but you can always use some cardio when you're going into the Rocky Mountains. The air is thin up high. I know Dan was putting in the work too. When he started, he was riding five miles, then ten, then more. I know when you tell someone you ride your bike thirty miles in two hours and fifteen minutes, they usually look at you funny, but it's not work for me. It's fun, and I enjoy every minute of it. And it's good for you. I can also say compared to running, it is much easier on your knees, hips, and back.

Dan told me that he was working on learning how to call an elk! He had bought a bugle and a cow call and was watching videos on how to use them. I can remember thinking, *How wild it would be for him to call in a bull for me on his first ever elk hunt.* We were keeping in touch, and I had sent him a list of things that he would need to acquire for the trip, and he was busy working on that list and making great headway. I think Liz, Dan's wife, was thinking, *How much stuff do you need to go elk hunting?* I told Dan the one thing good about buying it is that when you have it, you don't need to buy it again if you want to elk hunt again, and if you never elk hunt again, you have what you need to go camping and be comfortable. It's a win-win situation.

Meg got us hooked up with plane tickets, and Chuck was going to let us use and abuse his belongings again. I was looking forward to seeing him again and somewhere other than a hospital. Chuck said we would be using Moby again, and I was happy about that because old Moby can get you there when you need her too; I know that! Dan and I were keeping tabs on each other and buttoning up all of the fine details for the upcoming hunt. Dan had applied for a bonus deer tag and had been put on a list. As the general drawing had ended, any extra tags would be given out to people on the list in descending order until they were all gone. It was a long shot but me, I'll always take a long shot over no chance at all. Dan was going to buy wolf, mountain lion, fishing, and upland game bird licenses over the counter when we got there. I knew Dan would catch fish and get some grouse with his bow, and knowing Dan the way I do, I knew he would enjoy himself just going along and experiencing the mountains and everything Montana has to offer.

September arrived, and so did the day. Dan was driving down to my house in Columbus. Dan was driving down the day before the flight. It's always more fun to travel with someone. We had talked about flying separately, but Dan wanted to travel together so he was going to drive down and fly out of Columbus with me. That would also give us time to go through everything he had to make sure he had what he needed and didn't take stuff he wouldn't need. Dan had done a good job of getting what he needed. We made a few small adjustments, and he was all set to go.

We were scheduled on a later flight, which would put us into Missoula at 10:00 p.m. My sister Bonnie was going to pick us up at the airport and haul us up to Chuck's place where she would spend the night and then run around town with us the next morning while we got stocked up for the hunt. At that point, we would part company. We would go hunting, and she would go home because she goes back to Michigan every year for a get-together and wouldn't be around when we got out of the hills.

When we got into Missoula, Bonnie was waiting for us at the baggage claim area. We were met with a nice hug from her. I hadn't seen her since I was in rehab in Spokane a year ago.

Here is a quick fun fact about Spokane I want to share. There are turkeys running around the place! The time Meg, Karen, Bonnie and I went out for pizza, I saw them. I said "That's a turkey!" as I saw them walking across the road.

Meg said, "Oh yeah, they're everywhere."

So if you're ever in Spokane driving around, watch out for them!

We got our gear loaded up and drove up the Blackfoot to Chuck's place. When we got there, it was after eleven. The lights were on, but it didn't look as though anyone was around even though his van was in the driveway. Chuck left the door unlocked for us, so we knocked as we were walking in. We didn't see him anywhere, and as we made our way farther into his house, we found him asleep on his bed. We, of course, woke him up. I hadn't seen Chuck since the day he brought my gear to me in Spokane before we left to go home. We shook hands, and I gave him a hug, which I'm sure he hated, ha ha. I introduced Dan and Chuck. Bonnie and Chuck have known each other for years. We stayed up into the early morning, around two or so.

I said, "We got a busy morning. We should turn in and get some sleep." Everyone agreed and we all went to bed.

The daylight coming through the window woke me up. It was around seven. Chuck's place sits down in the Blackfoot River canyon and gets less daylight than other places. It's a very cool spot. You can see game across the canyon, on the east side of the river. Or you can see it right at Chuck's place. He has had a grizzly in his driveway before. It had been coming in and helping himself to Chuck's neighbors' chickens.

Chuck will leave his front door open when he's home, so it's probably a good thing he keeps a loaded 12-gauge shotgun handy. Chuck has told me about turkey, deer coming through his place as well as seeing elk on the hill behind his house. So in my opinion, he's in a great spot.

We were all up having coffee and a bite to eat. Chuck was getting ready to go to work. He told us Moby was "race ready," and we shouldn't have any problems with her.

He told us, "Good luck, and try not to have another trip like last year!"

We all laughed, and I said, "Believe me, one and done is my plan for trips like that!"

Chuck headed to work, and we left shortly after and headed down the canyon toward town. It was dark, and you couldn't see much other than the road when we went to Chuck's the night before. Now it was daylight, and Dan could see the scenery and was impressed with its beauty.

I told him, "I can't wait for you to see all of the places I'm going to take you." Montana is one great view after another.

We got into town and made our way to the sporting goods store. I picked up some fuel for my stove and some freeze-dry food. I also picked up a bottle of pine cover scent and a bow license, while Dan got what tags he could over the counter. Next, we went to the grocery store and got food for the week and plenty of water. We parted company with Bonnie. She headed home, and we headed back to Chucks to load up and head out.

We would be heading south to start the trip at my usual hunting spot. We were loaded up, fueled up, and headed south for the three-and-a-half-hour drive. A couple of hours into it, I looked over at Dan, and I don't think a plastic surgeon could have removed the smile from his face. I was wondering if anyone had been in there or would be in there. It seemed like there was always someone. If there was, I just hoped they wouldn't be in my favorite camping spot.

As we got off the paved road and started the nine-mile journey up into the hills on the dirt road, I was thinking that there may not be anyone in here for a couple of reasons. One, there wasn't any fresh tire tracks on the road, and two, there was a tree across the road about nine inches in diameter.

Dan said, "Oh man, what are we going to do now? Do you have a saw?"

I said, "I do. It may take us a while to cut through it, but if we run into something bigger, we may be out of luck! We took turns cutting on the tree and finally got it cut into manageable pieces and got them off the road. We high-fived, hopped back in, and started down the road again a short distance and came upon another tree down across the road. This one was smaller in size than the last one, but I was thinking, *If this keeps up, we may not make it into my spot with two trees down so close together.*

We cut that tree in half and moved it out of the way and continued on. We drove the final eight miles without coming upon another tree down on the road. I don't know how long the other trees had been down, but I do know that no one had been in there that day other than us.

I told Dan, "It could be good if no one's been in here for a while."

When we made it to the campsite, we got busy setting up camp. We pitched the tent, set up a nice firepit, and got a fire going, then continued to gather firewood for the night. I told Dan my plan for the next day, where we would be going, and how far we would hike. I let him know that even though it would be a long day, it wasn't a bad hike.

Dan said, "I'm up for whatever. I can't wait to go."

We just ate snacks for dinner and had a couple of beers enjoying the fire and each other's company. We got stuff around for the next day's hunt, then hit the hay.

CHAPTER 34

The alarm sounded off at 5:00 a.m., the way it had so many other times. We got up and out of our sleeping bags pretty quick. It was opening day after all! I was keeping an ear out for any bugles, or trucks that may be coming up from the valley. As we were getting breakfast of, you guessed it, oatmeal and coffee made, along with putting lunches together, we didn't hear any bugles, and I don't recall hearing any the night before while we were in the tent or by the fire. That was okay. I know there are elk around. Something else we didn't hear was anyone coming in from the valley, so we had the place to ourselves. We ate and filled up our water bladders, got our packs set along with our bows, walked across the road, and headed up the ridge.

We were walking along at a very slow pace in the darkness. I didn't want to bump into elk and spook them. As we ascended higher and higher, we made our way to the first opening, and I bugled. A bull answered across the draw, down on a lower ridge. It wasn't a quick response, but nonetheless, we had got a reply, and he was on the route we would be taking on our way back to camp. I called again, but he didn't answer this time. We were hunting in the wolf-infested area, so I wasn't surprised or concerned at the lack of response. We hiked higher and higher, and as morning turned into late morning, I told Dan to call down over the side of the mountain toward the bull we had heard earlier. Dan moved over to a tree and bugled.

I have to say for the first time hearing him bugle, it was a solid bugle. Dan bugled a second time, then he picked up a good-size stick and started to beat it up against a sapling that was there. So far, everything Dan had done sounded great. He was over there beating the tree to death, then he stopped, tossed the stick to the ground, and walked back over at his normal slow and steady pace. I was cracking up. Dan doesn't do anything at any other pace than his own.

I was recording the whole thing on my phone, and after the hunt, I was up in Michigan and showed the video to Dan's uncles, Dan and Tim. Tim said, "Boy, that's old Dan for sure. He does everything at his own pace."

We weren't seeing much fresh sign. You could tell the elk had been on that ridge, just not recently, maybe a week ago but no more than two, based on how dry the scat was we were finding. When we reached the top of the ridge and were on the one side of the saddle, we threw out a couple more bugles, hoping the bull would sound off but got nothing in return. We crossed through the saddle to the ridge above where the bull was at and bugled again. We got a bugle right back. It was from down over not too far away, but he called right back. We took our time, moving slowly to a position that would have us right above the bull. Once we made it there, I bugled, and the bull bugled right back from right below us. We took cover and prepared for an encounter. The morning thermals had shifted the wind in our faces, and we both were doing some soft cow calls and could hear the bull below us. We waited several minutes, and nothing. So I motioned for Dan to bugle again, and he did—nothing. I let him know we were going to hold tight in case the bull was coming in silent. We stayed set up for an hour but never saw or heard the bull again.

We made our way down the ridge, dropped off the side of it to the bottom, and worked our way back up to the ridge top we had gone up in the early morning and worked our way back down to camp. We got back to camp around three in the afternoon. I suggested we take a break for a little while and relax, then go road hunting for grouse later on toward evening. The grouse came to the road to get grit for their craw to grind up what they had been picking at all day, so walking or driving dirt roads in the mornings or evenings is a great way to find grouse in the mountains. Dan liked the plan.

We had some snacks and hydrated ourselves, relaxed for a bit, then fired up Moby and set out on our grouse hunt.

Grouse like to hang out in tight switchbacks that have a water source in them and so are great areas to run into them. The road camp is on. It has produced again and again for me in the past, and I was hoping she would again. We drove the entire road out to the end of it and saw nothing, but you never know. Maybe we were just early and would find them there on the way back. On the way back, we ran into one on the side of the road. I stopped Moby, and Dan got out, drew his bow, and released. The shot was true, and the arrow did its job. We knew we were having grouse for dinner. I was happy Dan got the bird, and based on the smile on his face, I'm pretty sure he liked shooting grouse with the bow. As we continued on our way back to camp, we were fortunate enough to run into a second bird and were able to secure that bird too, so we were going to get our fill tonight.

Once we got back to camp, I dressed the birds, and Dan went about cutting potatoes and onions up. I boned out the meat and sliced it into half-inch cuts. We had some heavy duty foil and double wrapped the meat and potatoes for fire cooking. We did the usual olive oil spray and seasonings on the meat and potatoes, wrapped them up, and waited for the fire to produce some good cooking coals. We were enjoying some ice-cold beverages and talked about the day's hunt as we waited for the fire to die down. We talked about the next morning and what the plan would be. The fire had some great cooking coals at this point, and we threw in the potatoes and got them cooking. I pulled a small pile of coals out of the main fire to cook the meat on. I was worried the main fire was still a bit too hot and wanted everything to finish cooking at the same time. I put the meat on top of the bigger coals and set some smaller coals on top of the foil and created our own mini oven for the meat.

The plan worked out perfectly. The meat was done and was really moist. The potatoes were cooked all the way through and golden brown with a little crunch to them. Some of the onions were burnt but not enough to matter to us. We ate every bit of it. Dan said he really liked the meal and hoped we got into the grouse again. I laughed. I think he was hooked. Evening turned into night as we sat by the fire and had a great time and conversation. Then we were off to bed. We would hunt down from camp in the morning as I usually did, hoping to catch the elk coming up from the valley to bed.

The alarm sounded, and we got up and dressed and were following the same routine as the day before, except we lingered at camp a bit longer than usual. I wanted it to be almost daylight when we accessed the ridge I wanted to hunt.

That ridge was the same ridge Dirsch had shot his bull on. We arrived at the ridge at the perfect time I would say. It was legal shooting time. We called and got a bugle right back from out on the ridge. The ridge had timber up where we were, and as you descended it, the timber gave way to open sage brush that continued down into the valley floor. The valley floor consists of wheat and alfalfa fields the elk feed on at night. The bull sounded like he was out in the sagebrush. Dan and I looked at each other and smiled. I told Dan we would just take our time and ease down the road so we didn't bump any elk and blow them out of there. We started down the road, and the bull bugled again. This time we could tell he was closer. It still sounded like he was out in the sagebrush. We made the edge of the timberline before the bull did. I had Dan hold back as I made my way to the edge of the cover.

I was standing by a little opening and asked God to help me out, *Where should I stand?* I looked over, and in my head, I was hearing, *Go stand by that tree.* So I moved over by the tree I had been looking at. This area was a secluded opening surrounded by trees and full of grass. I looked back at Dan and gave him the sign to call. Dan called, and the bull bugled right back. It sounded as if the elk had covered some ground and were at least parallel with me or even a bit higher up than I was. At that time, I readjusted my position from the tree to another tree about thirty yards farther up the ridge. I only went the short distance so I didn't run into the elk and set up again where I had some shooting lanes in a couple of directions. I could see movement coming my way through the trees. Then I could make out a big cow elk leading the way. She was moving from my left to my right toward, you guessed it, the little opening I had been set up in by the tree to start with. As the big cow made her way to the opening, I could see four more elk following her. All were slick heads, or cows, as some call them. Dan called again, and the bull sounded off really close. The first cow was now standing right in one of my shooting lanes broadside, wide open, and no idea I was around. I figured this was my one chance and started to pull back on the string, then I caught movement in front of me. It was the bull, a five-by-five bull, and he was following the same route as all of the other elk had. Each one of the elk had walked into my shooting lane and stopped twenty-four yards away, then walked into the opening I had been set up on to start with. I let up on the string, figuring the bull would walk right into the opening just as the rest of the elk had. The wind was perfect; it was coming from the elk toward me. The last cow had just moved out of the opening, and the bull was headed right toward it. I was wrestling with the old "bird in the hand" phrase, hoping the bull followed suit. He was walking the exact same path all of the other elk took and was almost to my shooting lane. I drew my bow as he walked behind a big tree, and instead of turning to the right and stepping into my opening, he continued straight into the open spot I had been set up on to start with and walked right out into the middle of it and stopped at forty yards.

I had no shot because the grass was so high in the opening, and he was a bit farther downhill then the rest had been. The grass covered up about three quarters of his chest, and I wasn't going to try to weave an arrow through it and wound the bull. Had I stayed where someone from above had told me to, it would have been over. Now I needed something to happen that would put him in an opening I could shoot to. By now, the cows had moved to our downwind side, and the bull was on his way to them. It was just a matter of time before they caught our wind, and they did just as the bull bugled one last time. A very cool encounter, and the bull gathered up his girls, and they moved off at a steady pace. They knew something was up but weren't too spooked. I had hope that we maybe could get out ahead of them and get another crack at them, but I was pretty sure that was my one and only solid opportunity for the trip, and my greed for the bull's antlers and not trusting my guide from above's direction was most likely going to cost me a freezer full of meat that would have fed my family for the year.

Dan and I met up, and I told him my side of the encounter and that he had done a great job of calling.

Dan said, "It's early. We will get into them again."

I said, "Like I said before, you usually get one solid chance during the week, and the cows were it. I passed on it because the bull was coming."

Dan said, "I think you did the right thing. If you have a bull coming, you have to see if it's going to work out."

I said, "Yep I did, and it didn't."

I was okay with the outcome. It was a great encounter, and Dan did a great job of working the bull. Who knew, maybe we would get into another bull. It was only the second day. I can tell you this, the next time I ask God for direction and get an overwhelming "Go stand by that tree!" you can take it to the bank my butt is going by the tree and staying right there. God doesn't make mistakes!

Dan and I hunted out the rest of the day without any more encounters and made our way back to camp without hearing another elk. It didn't matter; it was a great day of hunting and enjoying God's creation, and it was only day two with many more to go and plenty to do and to see. We got back to camp and got all of the gear squared away for the next day.

We took Chuck's archery target with us, and we were having a great time shooting our bows and talking about the day's events. We talked about going grouse hunting again and decided we would go. Dan had been checking the weather, and it looked like rain was inbound. Dan confirmed we had weather on the way. We hunted the same hunt as the night before but with different results. No matter, we got back to camp and began preparing for the oncoming storm.

The wind had picked up, and the phone indicated the storm would be approaching from the south, southwest. The tent was sitting facing north and south, so we decided to turn it ninety degrees so the storm wouldn't be blowing directly at the end of the tent. We got the tent reset, and even though it had a rain fly on it, we got my tarp out for another layer of protection from the storm. I checked around the tent's location for dead limbs above and for dead trees that may fall and be able to reach the tent. Everything looked good.

Dan and I were prepared well ahead of the storm. We had the fire going, and we had freeze dry for dinner since we got snubbed by the grouse. Darkness fell over the valley, and shortly after that, it began to sprinkle. We secured the fire and headed to the tent to seek refuge from the storm.

Once we got in our sleeping bags, the storm picked up in its intensity. You could hear it pounding the tarp in sheets of rain, and the tarp was being tested by the wind too. We were talking and yucking it up in the tent and listening to it rage outside, and somewhere along the way, we both drifted off to sleep. I woke up because my head was getting wet. I sat up, and when I did, my sleeping pad went down into a small depression, and I got soaked from the waist down. I let out a few colorful adjectives about my new situation.

Dan woke up and said, "What's going on?"

I said, "I'm soaked. Are you wet?"

He said, "No, not really."

We got our headlamps on and got a good look at our situation, which wasn't a good one. Even with the fly and the tarp up, we had taken in water—and a lot of it! The depression in the ground that was under me was full of water. The floor of the tent was acting as a pool liner and, apparently, was the only thing on the tent that was waterproof. My sleeping bag and my legs were soaked. Dan's side was pretty good. He had a small pool on his side, but it did not affect him.

We talked about getting out and going to the truck but figured that we would get completely soaked if we did that. The storm was still raging outside. As crazy as it sounds, we decided to stay in the tent till morning. I slid over as far away from the pool as I could get and did my best to ring out my sleeping bag. Once I got settled into my sleeping bag, it did actually warm up again, and I was able to fall asleep again. I think that both of us slept as still as we could the rest of the night in an effort to stay out of the pools of water.

When morning came, I was never so happy to get up and out of my sleeping bag and tent. The morning was breaking as the storm had moved off, and the clouds were breaking up and giving way to a beautiful blue sky and sunshine peeking through from time to time until they took over the entire sky. It was chilly.

We got over to the truck and got some coffee going. We were laughing about the night's events, then started to pull all of our stuff out of the tent to dry it out. After getting the tent emptied out, it looked like the water had been coming in the wall and floor area of the front of the tent and running downhill to the low spots. Our inflatable mattresses had kept us up out of the water. If I hadn't sat up, my legs probably would have never gotten wet, but when I did, my weight pushed it below the water surface in the depression, and the water flowed over the top. Chuck needed to get a new tent was my takeaway on the whole thing! How does he expect me to go hunting when I have to stay in a tent that leaks every time it rains?

We got a fire going and were warming our bones by it and talking about what to do. Earlier, I had let out that I had a plan. I talked about getting Dan to Montana, and that was playing out in real time now. The part I didn't share was I wanted to go back to where my accident had taken place. That was the other part of my plan. I had been thinking about that since I was in the hospital after I snapped out of my funk. That thought has consumed me! It had more to do with my drive to get healthy and in shape to hunt than the actual hunt did.

After talking about it, we knew there were elk in our area, and if we left, they would likely still be there if we came back. The spot where my accident happened was loaded with elk last year and has always been a good spot, so we decided that we would let our gear dry out and pack everything up and drive up to the other area that day. Once there, we would set up camp and hunt the next morning. It would most likely take us four hours to drive up there. We planned to leave around noon which would get us there with time to set up at the new spot and give us time to relax for a bit. We kept moving our stuff around from spot to spot to keep it in the sun and dry out. It was working, and the moisture rising up out of our gear looked like several small smoldering fires.

We ate and repacked everything including our backpacks for the next day's hunt and made sure our bows were in good shape and still on. We started the process of loading Moby up. I did wonder how the road out would be given the storm and the down trees we encountered on the way in. I had concerns; if a big tree had fallen across the road, we were stuck in there and going nowhere fast! It was late morning, and the tent, tarp, and our sleeping bags were finally dry. We packed the rest of that stuff up and took off.

I think we were both a little tired from the night's events, but when you're on the move in Montana, it is so beautiful it is easy to rally to the cause. You don't want to miss anything. As we snaked our way out of the mountains, we didn't encounter any downed trees, which was wonderful. We made the hard top road and put the hammer down, headed north.

When we reached the area where we were going, I just went in the way Dirsch and I had come out on "The Day" last year, so I didn't waste time by going the original way I had always gone, only to find they still hadn't fixed the road. I was wondering if I could or would remember the way in since my memory was a little suspect from time to time. I knew I was looking for a left-hand turn off of the road that went up into where we had broken down in Moby the year before. Things were looking familiar to me, and after a couple of miles, there was the road taking off to the left. We turned and continued on. It looked like the road, and it seemed to be bumpy enough to be the road from what I could remember. We were bouncing around inside of Moby like a couple of kids in a bounce house. As we drove higher and higher, I could see the spot below us across the valley where Dirsch and I had broken down and pointed it out to Dan and the path we followed to get up out of there and onto the road we needed. When we were about to the top, I recognized the ribbons on the trees and knew for sure this was the right road. And we were close to popping out on the road where Dirsch and I had camped. We hit the intersection and hung a left, came around the corner, and there was our firepit on the side of the road from the year before.

I told Dan, "This is where we camped last year. We're going to drive up to the parking spot and just camp up there. It will save us a little time in the morning."

He was good with that. Dan is just an easygoing guy who goes with the flow. We pulled up into the parking spot which is not flat, got out, and stretched out our legs for a minute. I considered going back down to the old campsite, but there was a road off the parking spot to the right, and we drove back there and found a nice wide flat spot in the road and decided to camp there.

We got out and started to get things set up. We were gathering rocks for the firepit and were pulling wood in to burn when it started to rain! Dan checked the weather, and it showed they were forecasting rain showers throughout the night. Well, that settled that right then and there for us. After the night we had just spent the night before in the tent with the indoor swimming pool, we made the decision to sleep in Moby for the night! With that decision, we also decided to drive back to the parking spot and get settled in there. We loaded all of the stuff back up on Moby and drove back to the parking spot.

Once there, I pulled Moby up onto the bank in the parking area so the front end was higher up than the back end. That way, when we recline the seats, we would be lying flat when it was time to go to sleep.

Dan and I had made a couple of sandwiches earlier in the day that we had with us in the cab. Dan was able to access TV with an app on his phone, so we were reclining in Moby, eating sandwiches and chips and enjoying a cold beer, while watching Monday Night Football. It was the Saints versus the Texans, with the Saints winning a close one. Man, we were really roughing it just like the night before. Well, maybe not like the night before.

While we were watching the game, an owl must have been able to see the screen on Dan's phone, and the movement caught its eye. The owl swooped down over the front end of the truck, and it glided over and perched on a tree that didn't look like it should have been able to hold the owl up, but it did. I snapped a picture of him sitting on top of that tree looking back at us wondering what was going on with what he thought was dinner, a very cool encounter for sure. Dan and I were having a great time and yucking it up quite a bit. After the game ended, we talked a bit more, then fell asleep.

CHAPTER 35

I was hoping we would hear some elk in the morning and was also hoping the place was still loaded up with them like it had been the year before. Time would tell. The morning was clear and cold, and all of the clouds had settled into the valleys. It was very reminiscent of the day from a year before when my brain blew up. It was chilly, and everything was wet from the rain, but you could tell it was going to be a beauty of a day. I was very optimistic about the day's hunt being a good one. The night before, we had thrown out some bugles but got no replies. I wasn't concerned about getting no replies because we had a lot of ground to cover, and the elk could be anywhere. We ate breakfast, packed up some lunch, grabbed our bows, and started hiking.

I was full of mixed emotions as we hiked into the area. I was excited to think about the possibility of taking an elk, and maybe a great one. I was happy to be spending time with Dan and hoping for a grouse encounter or two. The thought of getting into a cougar encounter knowing Dan had a tag in his pocket was also running through my mind. I don't like them, but with Dan having a tag, I could stand one more encounter.

I was also determined to get back to the spot where everything had happened. I needed to do that for myself to put closure to the event for me.

Dan and I hiked down the road and past the gate. We made the finger ridge and headed up the point of it to the top which would put us on top of the main ridge. Once we were there, we found the remains of my stack of rocks in the road scattered a bit, but no doubt they were the ones from the pile I had made. I pointed them out to

Dan. We let out a bugle and waited; nothing came back. We called again and waited. Same thing, no reply, so we continued on.

I was thinking about the pile of rocks, and Dirsch and I talked about them on our way out that day and how I knew it was the pile I made but didn't know at that point on that day. We hadn't gone much farther when I saw a familiar sight which changed my optimism on whether we would find elk today or not. It was a pile of wolf dung full of elk hair. Not far from there, we found another pile, then another. In all, on that one small ridge, we found five piles, all packed full of elk hair. Dan and I were pretty sure why we hadn't heard any elk responding to our calls.

None of the piles were fresh, but elk aren't going to linger about with wolves hunting them down and eating them daily. We weren't seeing any fresh elk sign at all as we hiked in the same way Dirsch and I had the year before. The further we hiked in there, the more the emotions were stirring inside of me.

As we hiked, and the day warmed up, the clouds started to rise up out of the valleys where they had spent the night, and they now had joined us at our elevation, reducing our visibility to fifty yards at best. I had been using a mountain to navigate off of, but when the fog rolled in, I lost track of it and was using my inner compass to get around. The fog lifted, and we were looking down into a valley, which I was expecting to be, just not one with power lines in it!

I was standing there looking down into that valley, and Dan said, "What are you looking at?"

I said, "I was expecting to be looking into a valley, just not one with power lines in it!"

Dan had an app on his phone and pulled it up. It was then that we could clearly see my inner compass was not functioning very well. The app showed that while we were hiking in the dense fog, I had walked in a circle, and we were looking into the valley Dirsch and I had driven up the first time we went in there, the same valley we broke down in.

I can tell you my inner compass was telling me I was walking in a straight line the whole time, and it had been an extremely long time since my inner compass had been off like that.

Based on what the phone was telling us to do, we headed off into a direction that felt completely wrong to me, but as the fog lifted, there was my mountain, the one I was using to navigate off of, right where it should be. Now that we were found again, we continued to hike up the ridge. We were still throwing calls out with no replies, and we were finding more and more evidence that the wolves had been dieting on elk for quite some time. It was becoming clear this hike was more about my return to the site of my event than about harvesting an elk, but you never know. As we were getting closer to the spot, we came upon where Dirsch had shot his bull. I told Dan the story about the encounter and pointed to where I had been calling from, where the bulls were at, and where Dirsch had been set up where he shot the bull the first time and where the bull was for the second and final shot.

It was hard to believe that an area that held so many elk—and we had so many encounters—was void of any sign that they had been there at all. After talking about that, we started to hike again, and we weren't far from the spot.

On the "Day," the big bull was on top of the ridge above the draw Dirsch had shot his bull in, and he was wound up. I'll never know why he was worked up like that, but I have since wondered if he had lost his cows to another bull in a fight. If that was the case, I can't imagine what the other bull could have looked like that took his harem from him because he was a brute. Whatever the reason for it, in the five days we had been in there, that day, he was the most vulnerable he had been.

We worked our way to the area below where the bull had been, and I slowed my pace. I told Dan, "We are close to where it happened. I can remember looking up and down the ridge before it happened, and this looks like the right area."

I started looking for the log I had been sitting on when the aneurysm ruptured. It may have fallen to the ground since then; who could know for sure. As I slowly walked the area looking for the log, Dan held back, giving me my space as I searched for the log. My mind was racing. I was flooded with emotions. My eyes were filled with tears, then I saw it. I stopped and stared at the log, afraid to approach it in fear of what had taken place there, but I had come here for that very reason. I slowly approached the log from the low end of it. I walked along it to the spot where I had sat down on that day and sat down in the same fashion I had that day. I had tears streaming down my face. I turned my head, looking down the ridge in the direction I was looking when the aneurysm burst. I could vividly remember that moment that it almost ended for me!

I was sitting in the spot where I was told that I should have fallen over dead by all of the doctors who had cared for me after the event. Yet here I was, still alive by the grace of God and the help of many skilled people. The date was September the tenth, four days shy of the one year anniversary of the rupture.

As I sat there, I thanked God for sparing me that day and for the extra time I have been given because of his endless love for me and his generosity. I remembered the deal I had made with him on the walk out. God had delivered on everything I asked him for. I had made a promise to God and myself. When I knew what he wanted me to do, I would make good on my end of the deal. God truly does work in mysterious ways. I never thought that when I started writing this, that this is what he wanted in return, but now I am certain that it is. Here's why.

This whole experience has brought me to have a much deeper and personal relationship with God, which is what he wants from all of us. I have always believed in God and had my relationship with him how I wanted it to be. I don't think he was satisfied with that, and now with the deeper and more personal relationship, it feels right, and I continue to work on it.

Meg has always had a relationship with God, and I believe that our girls now have a deeper relationship with God, which makes me happy for them and for God. I never miss a morning to thank God for letting me start another day, which I feel we all should do daily. There is no guarantee for any of us that we are going to finish out the day on any day. We assume we will because we always have, but as sure as I'm writing this and as sure as you're reading this, the day you don't get to finish is out there! You don't know which one it is, but God does. Be thankful for each one you get to start because you never know; that day may be the day!

I think about how many things could have happened on that day and since then that could have stopped me from getting to the hospital or being okay—having the aneurysm burst three and a half miles from the truck, being another ten miles up in the mountains, then forty more miles to the nearest hospital. The wheel on the truck miraculously did not come off with only two lugs left on the wheel and the nuts right out to the end of the threads. Then I heard the doctor say I should have fallen over dead on the spot and the chances of me making it were less than 1 percent and that I was still alive after having the artery in my brain burst and was able to talk and walk and function and make it out of the mountains. Also, Dr. Carlson was on vacation but was still in town, and he came in to do my surgery and told Karen I would be fine after it, with no doubt or hesitation. How could he have known for sure?

I also got switched from the doctor I was assigned to in Columbus to the one Meg wanted me to have without asking for that change. Ann told me that I was the highest functioning patient she had ever worked with after sustaining the injury I did, with no one else to compare me to. Dr. Gewirtz, being every bit the surgeon Dr. Carlson was, I made it through my second brain surgery in four months, with the doctor going to the middle of my brain and back out and nothing being wrong with me after that. That is an awful lot of coincidences to randomly happen in my opinion. Then there was the Chinese zodiac—"Use extreme caution when venturing into the high mountains; severe injury or death could occur"—that I printed off the day before I left on the hunting trip. There was also the woman I talked to the day Payten and I went for the bike ride who told me "You need to finish your book. God wants you to brag about him!" as she sat there reading the Bible. My journal that I read two days after running into the woman reading the Bible was Psalm 50:15, "And in the day of trouble call upon me and I shall deliver you, and you shall glorify me!"

The list is long and undeniable to me. I believe God wants me to share this story to tell everyone that he is real, that he loves us all, even a sinner like me and you and wants all of us to be with him in heaven forever. God tells us in the Bible that he will never forsake us and is always with us. In my time of need, I called upon him because I knew there was no one other than him that could save me from my fate, and he delivered me when I asked him to out of an impossible situation, and I want to glorify him with this book, to let everyone know he is real. He is here, and he is with you always. He is mighty and is the King of kings! He loves you and me—all of us. He wants you to seek him and have a relationship with him.

We aren't earthly beings with soul. We are spiritual beings with earthly bodies. This is not our forever home. That place is with the Father, Son, and the Holy Ghost, and that place will be the best thing any of us could ever imagine. Don't be of things of this world. They mean nothing. Love your family, your friends, and your enemies and pray for all of them. Read the Bible because as the lady said, "It is the truth!" Spend time with God. You have no bigger fan than him! May God bless you all!

ABOUT THE AUTHOR

Dana Kelley Bergman is a first-time author who has an amazing story to tell and wants to share it in hopes of helping others. He has worked in logistics for the last thirty years. Kelley and his amazing wife, Megan, live in Ohio and have two daughters—Preslie, who resides in Michigan with her husband, Kam; and Payten, who lives in Ohio too and is finishing up her studies at OSU this year.

Kelley has a love of the outdoors and many things related to the outdoors such as hunting, fishing, hiking, camping, and biking. He is also interested in art and, when he has time, likes to do paintings and carve walking sticks.

Kelley loves spending time with family and friends when possible, and he and Megan love to travel and spend time at the beach.

Printed in the USA
CPSIA information can be obtained
at www.ICGtesting.com
JSHW020330020823
45798JS00002B/7